ASSOCIATION FOR LIBRARY AND INFORMATION SCIENCE EDUCATION (ALISE)

BOOK SERIES

SERIES EDITORS
Jaya Raju, University of Cape Town
Dietmar Wolfram, University of Wisconsin-Milwaukee

ABOUT THE SERIES
The ALISE Book Series, published by Rowman & Littlefield (https://rowman.com/), addresses issues critical to Library and Information Science education and research through the publication of epistemologically grounded scholarly texts which are inclusive of regional and national contexts around the world.

ABOUT ALISE
The Association for Library and Information Science Education (http://www.alise.org) is a non-profit organization that serves as the intellectual home of faculty, staff, and students in Library and Information Science, and allied disciplines. It promotes innovation and excellence internationally through leadership, collaboration, advocacy, and dissemination of scholarship.

Titles in the Series:
The Information Literacy Framework: Case Studies of Successful Implementation, by Heidi Julien, Melissa Gross, and Don Latham
E. J. Josey: Transformational Leader of the Modern Library Profession, by Renate L. Chancellor

E. J. Josey

Transformational Leader of the Modern Library Profession

Renate L. Chancellor

ROWMAN & LITTLEFIELD
Lanham • Boulder • New York • London

Published by Rowman & Littlefield
An imprint of The Rowman & Littlefield Publishing Group, Inc.
4501 Forbes Boulevard, Suite 200, Lanham, Maryland 20706
www.rowman.com

6 Tinworth Street, London SE11 5AL

British Library Cataloguing in Publication Information Available

Library of Congress Cataloging-in-Publication Data

Names: Chancellor, Renate, 1965– author.
Title: E. J. Josey : transformational leader of the modern library profession / Renate Chancellor.
Description: Lanham : Rowman & Littlefield, [2020] | Series: Association For Library And Information Science Education (ALISE) book series | Includes bibliographical references and index. | Summary: "This book examines the life and career of librarian, educator and activist E. J Josey. During Josey's professional life, which spanned fifty-five years, he worked as a librarian (1953–1966), an administrator of library services (1966–1986), and as a professor of library science (1986–1995)"—Provided by publisher.
Identifiers: LCCN 2019041918 (print) | LCCN 2019041919 (ebook) | ISBN 9781538121764 (cloth) | ISBN 9781538121771 (epub) | ISBN 9781538158913 (pbk)
Subjects: LCSH: Josey, E. J., 1924–2009. | American Library Association—History. | Librarians—United States—Biography. | African American librarians—Biography. | African Americans and libraries. | Minorities in library science—United States—History—20th century.
Classification: LCC Z720.J75 C47 2020 (print) | LCC Z720.J75 (ebook) | DDC 020.92 [B]—dc23
LC record available at https://lccn.loc.gov/2019041918
LC ebook record available at https://lccn.loc.gov/2019041919

To my parents, Bobby and Viola Chancellor, who inspired my love for black history and taught me to be fearless

Contents

Acknowledgments

I would like to extend thanks to all those who so generously contributed to the work presented in this book. I am especially grateful to those who shared with me their thoughts, experiences, and recollections of E. J. Josey. Many thanks to the Rowman & Littlefield staff, especially my editor, Charles Harmon, who helped to bring this book into completion. I would also like to thank the ALISE Book editors, Dietmar Wolfram and Jaya Raju, who provided critical and important commentary and advice that also aided in bringing this book to fruition.

I had the opportunity to present early versions of this project in several settings, including the Association for the Study of African American Life and History annual convention in Birmingham, Alabama. I was invited by my colleagues in the Department of Library and Information Science at the Catholic University of America to present at our inaugural annual Bridging the Spectrum Symposium in Washington, DC. I am grateful to Kelly Navies, former collections librarian at the MLK Memorial Library who invited me to speak at the MLK Memorial Library during their monthly speaker series. The invitation by Heather Wiggins to present at the Library of Congress in Washington, DC, was thrilling. I was especially grateful that I had the opportunity to share Josey's story with relatives of Rosa Parks.

I am indebted to the American Library Association Archives, the Savannah State University Library, the University of Pittsburgh Archives, the Portsmouth Public Library, the Birmingham Public Library Archives, and North Carolina Central University School of Library and Information Sciences, who allowed me to spend endless hours viewing Josey's papers. I would be remiss without acknowledging the guidance of Blanche Woolls, who connected me with my editor, and thanking all of my research assistants who helped with editing, formatting, and fact checking iterations of the manuscript. I would like to thank friend and colleague Dr. Joan Lussky for her detailed attention and care with indexing this book.

Feedback from family, friends, and other scholars across the country helped me to reexamine my own conclusions and perspectives. I would like to thank my mother, Viola, whose love and guidance are with me in whatever I pursue; my sister, Heidi, who was often a sounding board for ideas and organization of this manuscript; my nephew, Isiah, who reviewed drafts and provided key input for adding color to Josey's story. I would especially like to thank Dr. Shari Lee for her endless and enthusiastic support during this entire journey.

Finally, I would like to thank E. J. Josey's family. I am extremely grateful for the support and kindness of Elaine Jacqueline Josey Turner and Lawrence Turner, who opened their hearts and home to me so that their father's story could be told.

Preface

Discourse on the contributions of African American librarians has been scant in library and information science (LIS) literature. In fact, it was not until I was enrolled in the historical research methods course in the penultimate quarter before receiving my master's in library and information studies that I stumbled across an article that referred to librarian Elonnie Junius Josey, affectionately referred to as E. J. Josey. I was thrilled but also disappointed that I had completed nearly two years of study without hearing about the contributions of not only African American librarians but other librarians of color. My excitement was quickly discovered by Professor Mary Niles Maack, who eventually convinced me to conduct a dissertation on Josey's life. I could never have imagined that the serendipitous article on Josey would lead to years of research and discovery on his life and leadership in the modern library profession.

Within the broader historical and political landscape of the civil rights movement, this work examines the life and professional career of E. J. Josey. In the era of Jim Crow, Josey rose to prominence in the LIS profession by challenging the American Library Association (ALA) to live up to their creed of equality for all. Using interviews with Josey and his contemporaries, as well as several primary and secondary sources, this book traces his life and transformative leadership in the modern library profession. During Josey's professional career, which spanned over fifty years, he worked as a librarian, an administrator of library services, and as a professor of LIS. He also served as president of the ALA in 1984–1985. He was very active in many professional associations in and outside of librarianship. His most notable achievement occurred in 1964 when he proposed a resolution that would prevent Southern library associations from discriminating against African American librarians.

This book will seek to answer the following question: In what ways did Josey transform the American Library Association? Central to this investigation are questions related to the impact of external historical factors of inequity, segregation, and the civil rights movement. Although Josey was a profound scholar who wrote extensively on his experiences and those of other librarians, this book aims to be a critical, comprehensive examination of his professional career. It expands on the festschrift written as a tribute to him and examines the life and leadership within a transformational leadership framework.

Much of the data gathered for this project was found in retracing his personal journey and rise to leadership. Travel to his hometown in Portsmouth, Virginia, and visiting the segregated neighborhood where he grew up—in Mount Hermon located in the Tidewater Region (also known at the Hampton Roads)—provided much insight into his humble beginnings. This southwestern section of the Commonwealth of Virginia includes cities such as Norfolk, (where Josey was born), Newport News, Portsmouth, and Chesapeake. Although the house where he was raised on Florida Avenue no longer stands today, many of his neighbors have vivid memories of him and his family in the community. It was fascinating to visit the renovated I. C. Norcom High School, where Josey attended and began to demonstrate early traits of leadership, and to meet with his fellow parishioners at Celestial Baptist Church, where Josey received his faith formation and spent so much of his time playing the organ. He continued his membership and kept in touch with his friends at Celestial long after he moved away. I went on to investigate Josey's journey by visiting the University of Pittsburgh School of Library and Information Science and spending time with his daughter, Amina Josey Turner (née Elaine Jacqueline Josey), and son-in-law, Lawrence Richard Turner III, in Greenville, North Carolina. In Washington, North Carolina, I had the opportunity to see the early development of the E. J. Josey Foundation for Justice and Peace.

Throughout this endeavor, I have had the pleasure of meeting and interviewing so many people who were inspired by Josey—both in and outside of librarianship. Josey had a tremendous impact on his childhood friends, his colleagues, and his family. Each person, whether friend or foe, had an interesting story to share about him. Each story helped shape this biography. In addition to interviews, considerable secondary sources were consulted, as well as documentary research. The ALA Archives located at the University of Illinois at Urbana-Champaign maintains a wealth of material in the form of meeting minutes, reports, and newsletters that document early civil rights efforts in the ALA. The information obtained was useful in identifying key individuals involved in ALA's civil rights movement as well as providing the background for developing questions used in interviews with Josey and his colleagues. Josey's professional and personal papers, including photographs, travel diaries, correspondence to the ALA, reports, and letters at North Carolina Central University School of Library and Information Sciences provided great insight into his thinking on many of the issues he advocated. The archives at the University of Pittsburgh, the University of Delaware, and Savannah State College were also helpful in understanding Josey's academic career and proved to be critical to this book. While this story is about Josey and his leadership in the ALA during a period of civil unrest in the 1960s, it is also a timely topic that is worthy of critical interrogation given modern-day racial polarization.

Josey blazed trails for hundreds of librarians whom he recruited to the profession and hundreds more who have serendipitously learned of his contributions. In many ways, the profession craves the enthusiasm, passion, vision, and transformative leadership that Josey brought to it. Many have argued that the same issues that were prevalent in the 1950s exist today. Others claim that things are much worse. Given the social and political landscape of today, it is very difficult to dismiss these sentiments. Several years ago, when I informed Josey that I would be writing a dissertation on his contributions to LIS, he was surprised. He immediately quipped, "I don't think I'm worthy of such an honor." As I reflect on that conversation today, now several additional years later, my response remains the same—yes, you are!

As a luminary in LIS, Josey's biography is needed in order to obtain an understanding of the role he played in catalyzing change in the profession. This work makes a significant contribution as it explores racial tensions and the struggle for civil and human rights in the profession. It also offers an opportunity to contextualize modern-day civil rights activities. The scope of this book will provide much interest and value to undergraduate and graduate African American studies and LIS students. It documents for the historical record a significant period of history that is underexplored in the scholarly literature. The intended audience for this book is researchers, historians, LIS scholars, and students. Josey's influence on the policies of the profession is of great significance today, as well as the future of LIS. Readers will be able to use his triumphs of leadership as a model for recruitment of students of color to the profession as well as advocacy on social justice issues.

The book is organized into six chapters that not only allow the reader to see the evolution of Josey's leadership, but it also offers a glimpse of the historical underpinnings of the modern library profession. Chapter 1 describes Josey's leadership journey and presents the theoretical framework as an analytical lens to examine his activism. Chapter 2 chronicles his childhood and early years. In chapter 3, we see Josey's early career as a librarian. Chapter 4 describes his efforts to dismantle discrimination in the profession. It also details his historic resolution that ultimately led to the integration of the ALA. Chapter 5 chronicles his leadership as an educator through his scholarship, teaching, and mentorship. The final chapter discusses Josey's legacy as a trailblazer in the profession.

Foreword

E. J. Josey was my father.

In order to do justice to my father's memory and to his unparalleled accomplishments in the field of library and information science, I had to do some research before writing the foreword to *E. J. Josey: Transformational Leader of the Modern Library Profession*. A father to a child is father first and *then* the public persona: the stature, the *fame* for which he may be known takes on a different form to the child. Actually, it takes second place in the order of importance.

Although my parents divorced when I was five at a time when divorce was still considered a taboo, and the children of divorce were described as "maladjusted," my mother made sure that I had a healthy ongoing relationship with my dad. I remember as a girl, sitting on his lap and smelling his cologne. I can still sense the tender way in which he informed me that my maternal grandmother had passed as we drove back during the holidays to my home in Philadelphia. Photos from the summer trips to Portsmouth, Virginia, his boyhood home, and to other places, such as Queens and Manhattan, New York; Wilmington, Delaware; and Baltimore, Maryland, to visit dear longtime family friends remain with me. The trips to the Philadelphia International Airport with my mother to pick up Dad for his visits still make me chuckle. It is a period piece, somewhat. Mother would slide from beneath the steering wheel for Dad to drive us home for a dinner filled with conversation about my school, NAACP, Martin Luther King Jr., John F. Kennedy, C. Delores Tucker, Cecil Moore, Roy Wilkins, and other names and events that I have probably forgotten but all were instrumental in my civil rights development and worldview. The book-signing parties in New York City held in the home of his distinguished colleague, Dr. Vivian D. Hewitt, and the many opportunities to travel to witness the awards and recognitions bestowed upon him by his beloved American Library Association are still fresh in my mind. Even my six children—his grandchildren—partook in some of these adventures with my dad, particularly my only son, Muhammed. All of these memories are significant in knowing who E. J. was.

Dad lived the life he espoused to others. He valued family, which is why I believe he created *community* for his students at Delaware State College,[1] Savannah State College,[2] and the University of Pittsburgh. He was forever mentoring, advising—the standard-bearer, the loving critic, and yet always the perfect listener and analyst. He was the educator and the student. He saw potential in all regardless of what may have appeared to others as deficits.

Indeed, a renaissance man—a man for all seasons—who read his Daily Word every day and had a number of favorite scriptures, one of which was *I can do all things through Christ which strengthens me* (Philippians 4:13 King James Version). A church organist in his younger years, he loved hymns, popular music, and favored classical music, and he respected the faith of others, having many friends and students of all persuasions.

Out of his 100 or more degrees, plaques, and accolades, the signatures affixed reflect the "who's who" of the twentieth century: Mordecai Johnson (Howard University); Dwight D. Eisenhower (Columbia University); President Bill Clinton (as governor of Arkansas); Congressman Louis Stokes (Ohio); Congressman Major Owens (New York); Marion Barry (Mayor of Washington, DC); Roy Wilkins (NAACP); Benjamin Hooks (NAACP); and so many others. His life exhibited an unwavering faith that empowered him to take stands that were unpopular, but spoke to universal truths. He was equally admired, loved, and hated, but always respected. As a librarian, the expectation was to catalog history. E. J. made history. History tells us that E. J. Josey's impact redefined the role of the black librarian as Charles Hamilton Houston reshaped the responsibility of the black lawyer. Dad was thoughtful, strategic, politically astute, and he demonstrated during the course of his prolific career a new paradigm, not only for the profession of library science but for other professional organizations to mimic in advocating for black Americans and for the rights of all minorities to be served and recognized as an important constituency in the American fabric.

In other words, E. J. Josey forged ahead to conscientiously democratize libraries, not only in America but throughout the world, and in so doing, he put the African diaspora on the map of the library world. In our current world, due to the reach of technology, the entire globe has become the librarian's zip code, while balancing local constituent needs and services. Of this, E. J. was aware, and he challenged the profession to remain true to this mission early on.

In 2007, the E. J. Josey Foundation for Justice and Peace conducted a host of open-call interviews during the American Library Association (ALA) Annual Conference in Washington, DC. For two days, former students, colleagues, past ALA presidents, and library professionals representing public, academic, and special libraries discussed the impact of E. J.'s leadership upon the profession, the association, and their professional practice. One former ALA president expressed admiration for his leadership in the integration of ALA, his influence over decades in the development and mentoring of women and minority library professionals, as well as E. J.'s courage and fearlessness. A former ALA councilor extolled E. J.'s leadership in the 1970s in the creation of an ALA Blue Ribbon Panel to investigate racism at the Library of Congress, exposing the working conditions for the library staff at this prestigious institution. One other former ALA president shared how often she referenced *Libraries, Coalitions, and the Public Good*, one of many books by E. J. Josey that reaffirms the public sector's responsibility in the support of public libraries.

E. J. was a man of principle and vision who advocated for human rights, for equal access to information, pay equity, academic freedom, and social responsibility—all of which are embodied in the noble ideals of equality, justice, and peace. I often wonder what Dad—E. J.—would say today, and all I have to do is to read some of his speeches from decades long ago. The parallels are astonishing, the themes familiar, and I can still hear his fierce voice of conscience, the eloquent, deliberate, modulated, scholarly presentation that made the Virginia son an American treasure and gift to the world for social justice and peace.

From the archives of the E. J. Josey Foundation for Justice and Peace, on a yellowed steno-pad page Dad penned this:

> It would be wonderful, if we did not need the black Caucus, REFORMA, the Chinese Librarian Association, the American Indian Library Association, the Jewish Caucus, and the Asian Pacific Library Association, but [members of Council,] racism is still endemic in American society. I hope that in our lifetime that we can have a country that will reflect a real cultural diversity, which will ensure equal access, equal opportunity, and full freedom for all American people.

Amina Josey Turner (née Elaine Jacqueline Josey)
April 2019

NOTES

1. Delaware State University in Dover, Delaware.
2. Savannah State University in Savannah, Georgia.

Chapter One

Journey toward Leadership

Driven by the desire "to destroy the barriers which divide white men from black men,"[1] E. J. Josey embarked on a journey of activism in the American Library Association that would last more than five decades. He was instrumental in promoting library science as a career for African Americans, and ensuring that they received equal opportunities in libraries and state and national professional associations. Armed with his early grounding in family and church in the rigidly segregated South of his youth, Josey overcame many economic and racial challenges. The path to equality was not always easy for him, but with the support of his family, and his own tenacious spirit, Josey exhibited strong leadership early in life. This was accomplished largely because of those earlier experiences. He went on to take on several key roles in the profession. Although he was beloved and lauded by many as a great leader in library and information science (LIS), it is important to understand the extent of his leadership. Therefore, Bernard Bass' theory of transformational leadership will be used as a framework to examine Josey's fifty-year activism in the modern library profession.

Josey's first leadership role occurred unexpectedly when his father passed away when he was a sophomore in high school. He completed his studies early so that he could help support his family. He earned money playing the organ at neighborhood churches and was later drafted into the army during World War II (WWII). While stationed at the army camps in the South, he served in segregated units and encountered overt racism that would perpetually change his life. After serving three years in the army, Josey was honorably discharged and enrolled at Howard University, where he first majored in music and took advantage of the GI Bill, which provided an education benefit for veterans pursuing college, graduate school, or a training program. Upon graduation, Josey moved to New York and enrolled at Columbia Uni-

1

versity's master's program in history. He received a master of arts degree and began working at the journalism library at Columbia University where he met a librarian who encouraged him to pursue librarianship. After earning his degree in library science in 1953 from the State University of New York (SUNY) at Albany, he held several positions in libraries, including the Free Library of Philadelphia, Columbia University Library, and the New York Public Library. It was in New York when Josey began to get politically involved in the fight against racism. He joined a chapter of the National Association for the Advancement of Colored People (NAACP) and became active in the civil rights movement. His venture in eradicating injustice through a national organization later propelled him to fight for justice in the ALA.

In 1966, he was appointed bureau chief in the New York State Education Department Library, a post he held for eight years until he was promoted to bureau chief specialist of library services in the department, where he worked until 1986. Upon his departure from New York, he accepted a tenure position at the University of Pittsburgh School of Library and Information Science, where he taught courses on academic library management, with an emphasis on the organization and management of college research libraries. As a professor, Josey used his role to help mentor and recruit students to become librarians and library educators.

Throughout his career, Josey was involved in professional associations and held many offices, including chair of the Cultural Minorities Task Force of the National Commission on LIS and membership of the ALA Committee on Pay Equity, the ALA Committee on Legislation, and the ALA International Relations Committee. He was also active in human rights issues outside librarianship. He was a member of the NAACP for more than forty years and served as a faculty advisor to the Savannah, Georgia, chapter.

As the second African American to become president of the ALA, Josey was among a small number of blacks to pursue the profession of librarianship. This biography not only documents his life as a librarian, but it also highlights the historical struggle of racial tensions in the library profession. Josey's legacy in the field of librarianship is evident in the policies that he initiated and implemented through his committee work, his ALA presidency, and his accomplishments as a librarian. He is the recipient of numerous honors and awards for his achievement in the association. He has been recognized by several universities because of his commitment to librarianship and has received several honorary doctorates. In 1973, an honorary doctorate of humane letters degree was conferred on Josey from Shaw University. The University of Wisconsin-Milwaukee conferred the doctor of public services in 1987, North Carolina Central University honored him with the doctor of humanities in 1989, Clark Atlanta University bestowed upon him the doctor of letters degree in 1995, and Clarion University of Pennsylvania honored him with the doctor of humane letters in 2001.

He is also the recipient of the ALA Equality Award and the Martin Luther King Jr. Award, given by the ALA, for distinguished community leadership. In 1996, Josey's name was included on the ALA's Fiftieth Anniversary Honor Roll in recognition of his fundraising and lobbying efforts on behalf of the nation's 116,000-plus libraries. In 1999, at the ALA Midwinter Meeting, Josey was honored for his contribution to intellectual freedom on the Celebration of the thirtieth anniversary of the Office of Intellectual Freedom. In 2002, he received the highest honor from ALA—honorary membership for recognition of his "outstanding contributions of lasting importance to libraries and librarianship."[2] His plaque read:

> In recognition of his lasting contributions to library and information science, his tremendous influence in library education and recruitment, his tireless efforts and dedication to equality and social justice, and his long and distinguished career as a librarian, author, teacher, and mentor, Dr. E. J. Josey be awarded the highest honor this Association can bestow, Honorary Membership in the American Library Association.[3]

Longtime colleague Barbara Ford describes Josey and his abilities as a leader: "I think he leads from a high moral ground with very strong ideas that are based in strong values that are very important to the profession. At the same time, he's a very good listener, he is open to change, he's inclusive in allowing people to have their say; try to come to consensus while not compromising his principles."[4]

The concept of transformational leadership originated with James Downton in 1973 and was expanded on by James MacGregor Burns in 1978. In 1985, the concept was further developed by distinguished professor of leadership, Bass.[5]

Transformational leadership conceptualized by Bass will be used to demonstrate how Josey employed the tenets of idealized influence, intellectual stimulation, individual consideration, and inspirational motivation to lead students, information professionals, and his fellow colleagues in the library profession. The focal argument of this book is that Josey was a transformative leader—one who fought institutional and racial barriers to bring equity to the profession he so loved.

From an epistemological perspective, leadership studies include a variety of definitions and research methods.[6] Bass once famously wrote, "There are almost as many different definitions of leadership as there are persons who have attempted to define the concept."[7] In his landmark study, *Leadership*, Burns argued that transformational leadership occurs "when one or more persons *engage* with others in such a way that leaders and followers raise one another to higher levels of motivation and morality."[8] Furthermore, he asserts that a transformational leader is one who can guide, direct, and influence others to bring about a fundamental change; both externally and through internal processes.[9] He also contends that an effective leader is a change agent because of the ability to transcend self-interest in a way that results in individual and group transformation. Qualities of transformational leadership include (a) idealized influence, where the leader becomes a role model; (b) inspirational motivation, where the leader provides meaning and challenge through team spirit; (c) intellectual stimulation, whereby the leader takes a creative and innovative approach to invoking change; and (d) individual consideration, where the leader serves as a mentor to those whom he or she aspires to lead. Each tenet of this leadership theory is important in understanding Josey's prominence as a leader.

IDEALIZED INFLUENCE

A central component of *idealized influence* is the degree to which leaders act in admirable ways that cause followers to identify with them. One of the reasons Josey was so successful in leading change in the ALA was because he was highly respected and became a role model to so many librarians. Long before his activism on the issue of race in the profession, he had shown leadership on several committees and developed a reputation for being a hard

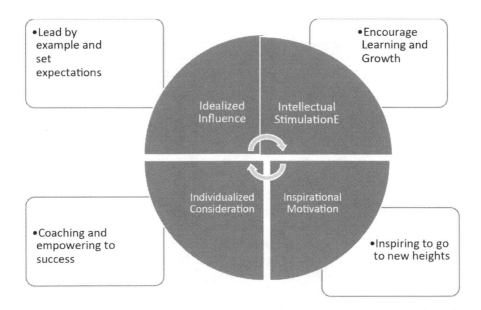

Figure 1.1.   Transformational Leadership Model. *Source: Bernard Bass*

worker and someone who possessed a high degree of integrity. Known for always wearing a suit, he presented himself like a leader, which demanded the admiration and respect from many of his colleagues. "I was so impressed with Dr. Josey's eloquent presentation, immaculate attire, and cool, dignified stature that I wanted to be like him. I knew that I wanted to be a librarian now, more than ever,"[10] remarked Malikah Dada Lumumba after attending one of Josey's talks at a Westchester Library System in the late 1960s.

Josey displayed his convictions and was not afraid to take a strong stand against issues he believed were in opposition to the core belief of democracy. He had an innate ability to appeal to followers on an emotional level. Al Kagan remarks, "[Josey] was extraordinarily effective as a leader. He was a very assertive person, and I would say commanded a lot of respect but also he had a lot of authority from the work he had done and his reputation."[11] Josey often used his charisma to influence individuals to follow the principles of democracy and justice. "He was a moral force from issues around the United States to around the world. He was all out there and leading us and showing us the way," Kagan said.[12]

Josey's charismatic nature commanded the attention of those around him. Because he demonstrated strong values, he became a role model for his followers. Joyce Wright was greatly influenced by Josey when she embarked on a career in librarianship. She was first introduced to him by Josey's mentee, Marva DeLoach, who encouraged her to pursue a library science degree. Wright considered Josey a role model and his work a positive example of conducting research at the highest standards. She further asserts that he was not only a role model to her but to countless other librarians. "Professor Josey has been a wonderful person, a role model, and a friend to so many Black professional librarians."[13]

There were times when Josey's advocacy provoked resentment. Much more often, however, his openness to differing points of view and his sincere searching for what was ethically right and wise for the association paved the way for a resolution of differences. Josey believed strongly that as a role model he was responsible for promoting democracy. "As someone who experienced discrimination firsthand and witnessed the injustices in society, I felt that it was important to encourage others, especially librarians, that they have an obligation to stand up to against [sic] injustice as well."[14] Moreover, Josey felt honored to be considered a role model for so many librarians. "I believe that if you treat people right, and act responsibly, then everyone has the potential to be a role model. . . . I have been blessed to be considered a role model from so many outstanding people in this great profession."[15]

Organizational scholars David A. Nadler and Michael L. Tushman contend that the strongest components of charismatic leadership are envisioning, energizing, and enabling.[16] These are very important aspects of Josey's transformative style of leadership that are attained not by controlling followers but by empowering them. Josey not only identified a problem that demanded great vision and spiritual commitment but was also fraught with danger and conflict. He demonstrated an individual and legitimate interest in eradicating racism within the profession, and his vision was expressed with the highest level of ethics and personal morals. Josey's positive experiences and team projects with leaders within ALA not only emboldened African American librarians but also contributed to Josey's own confidence in aligning himself with the twentieth century. Colleagues saw Josey as a person who was a visionary and had extraordinary ethical decision-making ability. He can best be characterized by Clara Stanton Jones, the first African American female president of the ALA, who asserts that "E. J. Josey's dynamic role in the [ALA] places him in the company of the great leaders in the history of American librarianship."[17] Former ALA president Barbara Ford believes this is Josey's greatest contribution to the profession:

> I would say serving as a role model and mentor for so many librarians through the years. Librarians from all kinds of backgrounds with all kinds of interests; he was always willing to talk with you to give you his best advice and opinion, and you know all people who reach the levels that he did; ALA presidency and the position he had in the New York State and at the University of Pittsburgh; not everyone is that open. But E. J. really took that mentoring, recruitment role very, very seriously, and I think that probably has the most impact and that's probably the least documented, I would say. Because it's easy to see what he did as president; you go to the archives and you pull it up. But the many people whose lives he touched, I think if there's as many of those that you can document, would be very, very important because he was such a personable person who you really felt cared about you.[18]

Just as great leaders like Martin Luther King Jr. and Marcus Garvey were role models to Josey, he was a role model to many for most of his life. Much of this has been substantiated in the findings that have been presented thus far. As a child growing up, Josey was a role model for his younger siblings as well as several of his friends in Portsmouth, Virginia. And, as an adult, he spoke out on numerous issues that many socially minded individuals opposed. His willingness to champion these causes allowed him to rise to prominence. However, it was not only his success in fighting for civil rights that garnered him notoriety, but, for many individuals, it was his ability to influence and energize them.

INSPIRATIONAL MOTIVATION

A leader in his own right, Sanford Berman was inspired by Josey and offers insight into what he perceives to be Josey's strongest attributes. "I can say without question that he was very much like my consciousness in my knowledge and as a paragon of and a flight of personal and professional virtue and high ethics and principle and perseverance."[19]

Josey was an inspiration to the many librarians he worked with in the profession. Starting with his return to Savannah State College as director of the library in 1959, Josey's professional life began in earnest. His tenure at Savannah State included establishing several major programs that made the institution into more of a center of intellectual life for the campus community.[20] Josey is credited with bringing white students to the Savannah campus for the first time in its history. He was able to persuade not only those in the black academic community to use the campus library, but he reached beyond the campus and was successful in influencing others to see the value in using the library. He also attracted renowned black writers and activists, like James Baldwin, to visit the campus library to speak to students about their literary works and cultural experiences. During this same time, Josey became an ardent supporter of student activist groups and was not only greatly impressed with the demonstrations that took place in Savannah, he encouraged students to be involved. Inspired by their efforts to fight for change, he used a similar approach to inspire others in the profession to combat racism.

Josey's motivation was also the driving force behind the establishment of the ALA's Black Caucus (BCALA). The caucus and his call for a plan to move the association forward to deal with the identified problems. The caucus was successful in having the ALA Council pass a resolution "that the librarians and/or librarians who do in fact, through either services or materials, support any such racist institutions be censured by the American Library Association."[21] As a leader of the first established ethnic caucus, Josey became an inspiration for other ethnic librarians to start their own caucuses. Over the years, BCALA has defended its members in court against discrimination. They have also built coalitions with diverse ALA groups, including the Asian American Caucus, the Chicano Task Force of the Social Responsibilities Round Table, and the National Association to Promote Library Services to the Spanish-Speaking (REFORMA). Implicit in a leader's ability to motivate and inspire his/her followers is trust. In organizing and building coalitions in the ALA, Josey was able to create trust among his constituency of black librarians as well as partnering and teaming with others throughout the ALA.

INTELLECTUAL STIMULATION

Intellectual stimulation is the extent to which a leader challenges assumptions, takes risks, and solicits followers' ideas and stimulates and encourages creativity in their followers. As the author of more than four hundred articles and thirteen books, Josey not only challenged his audience to elevate their minds to think along the lines of human and civil rights, but he provided librarians opportunities to publish their views as well. He mentored and encouraged aspiring authors to write on a myriad of issues pertaining to librarianship. As a result, he empowered the ALA by helping others contribute to it.

Another aspect of *intellectual stimulation* is the degree to which the leader attends to each follower's needs, acts as a mentor or coach to followers, and listens to their concerns. This also encompasses the need to respect and celebrate the individual contribution that each follower can make to the team—it is the diversity of the team that gives it its true strength. Josey actively engaged in mentoring and recruitment because he believed that "there is a dire need for more people of color to enter the profession of library science . . . [if they do not, our] 'multicultural society . . . will not have enough librarians of color to serve groups which are becoming the majority in America.'"[22] Josey also extended himself to people of color in the profession. "He has always been there as a guiding light, a person with integrity if you need help with something." Clara Chu, director of the Mortenson Center for International Library Programs, recalls being contacted by Josey when she was a new professor at UCLA: "[Josey] heard of my struggles with the challenges of being a professor and my tenure process. I received a letter of encouragement from him out of the blue offering me his help and/or support if I needed it."[23] She further stated, "I was personally moved that he would reach out to me, and it speaks to the type of person he is and how much he cares about people of color, particularly in the academic side of the profession."[24]

Josey was also critical of librarianship and the profession. He once chastised the ALA, declaring, "We care more about intellectual freedom than we do about human freedom or human aspirations."[25] Josey committed himself to right this wrong and emerged as a leader of his profession and community.

INDIVIDUAL CONSIDERATION

Individual consideration is where the leader serves as a mentor to those whom he or she aspires to lead. Josey's focus on recruitment and mentoring demonstrates the depth to which he was concerned about the future of the profession. His mentoring—through teams, interpersonal relationships, teaching, and a lifelong commitment to recruitment—are examples of his strong leadership. Josey's impact on others was documented in a tribute to him compiled by Ismail Abdullahi; these statements stand as testimony to Josey's leadership and service.[26] Mark Winston believes that "Josey was successful as a leader because he was able to recruit others to take on leadership roles."[27] Winston was greatly influenced by Josey's leadership and built his research around the general theme of leadership.

Throughout his career, Josey operated as an agent of change, proposing and then executing initiatives and policies at Delaware State College Library and Savannah State College Library that promoted library services and achieved unprecedented success with outreach to the faculty, students, and the surrounding community. As the chief of two bureaus in the Division of Library Development of the New York State Library in Albany, he helped implement the interlibrary loan system and ensured universal access to materials for academic libraries. Josey clearly exceeded the standards and expectations of his superiors by strengthening the overall pattern of library service in the state. One former colleague, Robert B. Ford, wrote that "as a supervisor, he had to possess good personnel management skills in terms of recruiting staff and motivating his subordinates. E. J. was quite successful in this area because of his good interpersonal skills."[28]

Not only did Josey pioneer change in working environments, but he was also a transformative leader in the ALA. The events of the civil rights movement best illustrate the indifference of the library profession to racial issues prior to the 1950s and 1960s. Josey recognized the need for an urgent transformation and challenged leaders in the ALA to address these issues. He frequently used his writings to convey his thoughts and views on topics he regarded as crucial to the advancement of equality in the library profession. Josey's legacy is his commitment to civil rights within librarianship and is matched only by his dedication to the broader movement for human rights in society. The biggest testament to Josey's role as a leader has been his ability to mentor others. This is best exemplified in the fact that so many other leaders consulted him and viewed him as a source of information. As mentioned previously, Josey was often sought out for his opinion on professional and personal matters.

In modern library history, few individuals have possessed the ability to inspire and elevate people to a higher level of consciousness. Josey was successful in this endeavor because of his tenacity and his unique ability to sway people, not merely by words but through action. The core belief that underlies all of Josey's actions was that libraries and librarians are important contributors to the American dream, one that envisions a racial, ethnic, and linguistic diversity. He was able to influence those in the ALA by appealing to the idealism of its members.

Josey captured the hearts and minds of his followers with his rhetoric as well as his irrepressible hope and optimism. He recognized the ongoing racism in the library profession and was able to communicate this in a way that resonated with the majority white population of the ALA. Josey learned how to converse with his colleagues across racial boundaries and made use of his own experiences with racism to emphasize the seriousness of the problem. Thus, his influence could be attributed to the fact that he won success, not just by gaining the support of African American and other ethnic librarians but by also appealing to the larger constituency of the organization.

Research examining the leading roles that African Americans have played in promoting civil rights and activism in the ALA is confined to brief narratives or to articles that do not fully analyze the work of significant individuals. This book fills a significant gap in the scholarly literature. Bass' theoretical framework not only provides an analytical lens to examine Josey's leadership behavior, but it also serves as an investigative apparatus to determine his effectiveness as defined by his contemporaries. Josey's leadership strategies, successes, and failures are analyzed using models drawn from leadership studies. Specifically examined are his accomplishments and how his legacy is a direct reflection of the events and people who helped shape his personal and professional life.

In June 2018, at the ALA Annual Conference in New Orleans, Louisiana, the ALA proposed a resolution that apologized for years of segregation in libraries. The resolution had several premises; however, one specifically recognizes Josey for his tireless effort to fight segregation:

> Whereas, despite the work of African American librarians, including but not limited to Clara Stanton Jones, E. J. Josey, Albert P. Marshall and Virginia Lacy Jones, and the allies who stood with them to fight segregation, a large majority of the nation's library community failed to address the injustices of segregated library services until the 1960s. [29]

This resolution not only underscores the crucial role Josey had in advocating for equality in the profession, but it also illuminates ALA's unwillingness to address the issue of race, so much so that more than fifty years later, the association is still grappling with their decision to be silent. Perhaps it is because many of these issues remain unresolved in 2019. While there has been progress on the racial front in the United States, many African Americans and other marginalized groups are still confronted with racism at work, in public spaces, and in countless sectors of society. They are victims of unarmed deaths while in police custody, racial profiling, and harassment by employees in public businesses like Starbucks.

This chapter describes Josey's leadership journey and presents a theoretical framework as an analytical lens to examine his activism. Throughout the remaining chapters, the story of Josey's rise to leadership will be presented. It will provide understanding of his motivation and the efficacy of his leadership. "I am not sure what has impelled other men to action in librarianship, but for me, it was a combination of my desire to make the library a more viable institution," said E. J. Josey when asked about his reasons for leading change in the profession. [30] It was not only his desire to make the library more viable for others by breaking down racial barriers that made him an effective leader, but it was also his charisma—his ability to motivate and galvanize others.

NOTES

1. E. J. Josey, "A Dreamer—with a Tiny Spark," in *The Black Librarian in America*, ed. E. J. Josey (Metuchen, NJ: Scarecrow Press, 1970), 323.

2. E. J. Josey, in personal communication with the author, April 10, 2007.

3. American Library Association, "Honorary Award of Membership," 2002.

4. Barbara Ford, personal interview with the author, April 9, 2007.

5. Bruce J. Avolio, "Bernard (Bernie) M. Bass (1925–2007)," *American Psychologist* 63, no. 7 (October 2008): 620, doi:10.1037/0003-066x.63.7.620.

6. Kem M. Gambrell, Gina S. Matkin, and Mark E. Burbach, "Cultivating Leadership: The Need for Renovating Models to Higher Epistemic Cognition," *Journal of Leadership and Organization Studies* 18, no. 3 (August 2011): 308–19, http://doi.org/10.1177/1548051811404895; Melissa Horner, "Leadership Theory: Past, Present and Future," *Team Performance Management: An International Journal* 3, no. 4 (1997): 270–87, http://doi.org/10.1108/13527599710195402.

7. Bernard M. Bass, *Bass and Stogdill's Handbook of Leadership: Theory, Research, and Managerial Applications*, 3rd ed. (New York: Free Press, 1990), 11.

8. James MacGregor Burns, *Leadership* (New York: Harper & Row Publishers, 1978), 20.

9. Bernard M. Bass, "From Transactional to Transformational Leadership: Learning to Share the Vision," *Organizational Dynamics* 18, no. 3 (Winter 1990): 21, https://doi.org/10.1016/0090-2616(90)90061-S; Burns, *Leadership*, 20.

10. Malikah Dada Lumumba, "E. J. Josey: A Mentor and Friend," in *E. J. Josey: An Activist Librarian*, ed. Ismail Abdullahi (Metuchen, NJ: Scarecrow Press, 1992), 155.

11. Al Kagan, personal interview with the author, April 9, 2007.

12. Kagan, personal interview with the author, April 9, 2007.

13. Joyce Wright, in discussion with the author, April 11, 2007.

14. E. J. Josey, in discussion with the author, January 7, 2004.

15. Josey, in discussion with the author, January 7, 2004.

16. David A. Nadler and Michael L. Tushman, *Competing by Design: The Power of Organizational Architecture* (New York: Oxford University Press, 1997).

17. Clara Stanton Jones, "E. J. Josey: Librarian for All Seasons," in *E. J. Josey: An Activist Librarian*, ed. Ismail Abdullahi (Metuchen, NJ: Scarecrow Press, 1992), 1.

18. Ford, in discussion with the author, April 9, 2007.

19. Sanford Berman, in discussion with the author, April 26, 2007.

20. Ismail Abdullahi, ed., *E. J. Josey: An Activist Librarian* (Metuchen, NJ: Scarecrow Press, 1992).

21. E. J. Josey, "E. J. Josey," in *Notable Black American Men*, ed. Jessie Carney Smith (Detroit, MI: Gale Research, 1999), 671.

22. "Library Pioneer Dr. E. J. Josey Saluted during American Library Assn. Annual Confab," *Jet* 88, no. 10 (July 1995): 33.

23. Clara Chu, in discussion with the author, June 19, 2008.

24. Chu, in discussion with the author, June 19, 2008.

25. Evan St. Lifer and Corinne Nelson, "Unequal Opportunities: Race Does Matter," *Library Journal* 122, no. 18 (November 1997): 43, http://proxycu.wrlc.org/login?url=https://search-proquest-com.proxycu.wrlc.org/docview/196736670?accountid=9940.

26. Abdullahi, ed., *E. J. Josey.*

27. Mark Winston, in personal communication with the author, July 3, 2008.

28. Robert B. Ford, "A Pioneer in a State Library Agency: The New York Years, 1966–1986," in *E. J. Josey: An Activist Librarian*, ed. Ismail Abdullahi (Metuchen, NJ: Scarecrow Press, 1992), 42.

29. American Library Association, "Resolution to Honor African Americans Who Fought Library Segregation," accessed May 22, 2018, www.ala.org.

30. Josey, "A Dreamer—with a Tiny Spark."

Chapter Two

A Dreamer with a Tiny Spark

Motivated by his lifelong pursuit to respond to the inequitable social conditions experienced by blacks, which were created by slavery and exacerbated by racism, E. J. Josey is best understood within the context of events, places, and time. To this end, an appreciation of the reality of his life offers an illumination of the spark of Josey from dreamer to transformative leader.

To be black in the United States, especially during the first half of the twentieth century, was to be alternately encouraged and disillusioned. In 1914, the migration of approximately 500,000 blacks from the agrarian South to the industrial North ultimately changed the social, cultural, and political landscape of cities like Chicago, New York, Pittsburgh, and Detroit. What was called the Great Migration transformed not only black America, but the entire nation.[1] Meanwhile, lynching, Jim Crow,[2] race riots, and overdiscrimination prevailed in the nation.

The decade of the 1920s—commonly referred to as the Roaring Twenties—was marked by renewed prosperity and opportunities for the United States in the aftermath of World War I (WWI). At first, the United States remained neutral in the conflict between Germany and its allies and Great Britain, France, and their allies. At this time, African Americans were not particularly welcomed in the segregated military services. The estimated 400,000 black Americans who enlisted or who were drafted represented about 10 percent of the US forces. Only about 50,000 saw combat; the majority worked in labor battalions, loading and unloading ships, building fortifications, and burying the battlefield dead.

This period was an especially significant turning point for African Americans, economically and intellectually. After nearly 350,000 blacks served in the armed forces in WWI, an excess of jobs became available in the industrial North where higher wages were paid to factory workers and miners. Spanning the decade, the Harlem Renaissance (also known as the Negro Renaissance) was "a cultural movement marked by increased literary, music, and artistic creativity by black artists who wanted to challenge the previous stereotypical representation of their image."[3] These leaders focused on proving the humanity and equality of African Americans and portrayed blacks as awakening from the dark days of oppression to the dawn of a new day of opportunity.

The Harlem Renaissance opened the doors of opportunity to black Americans in roles that had once been unreachable. Blacks became educators, best-selling authors, diplomats, internationally acclaimed celebrities, and librarians. The Harlem Renaissance revitalized American culture, yet despite these successes, the "New Negro"[4] still fell short of what they wanted most: equality. For the first time, African Americans had a chance to express themselves creatively and intellectually. The Harlem Renaissance produced many firsts: the first black to have a best-selling novel, the first African American woman to graduate from Columbia University, and entrepreneur Madam C. J. Walker, who is considered by many the first female self-made millionaire in the United States.[5] These pioneering efforts opened the door for other blacks and influenced an entire generation of emerging professionals and artists.

It was in this decade of great progress and growth that Josey was born. This age of unprecedented success for African Americans during the early years of Josey's life set the stage and became the foundation for his efforts to fight and overturn racial discrimination in society. He followed in the footsteps of great leaders like Jamaican-born Marcus Garvey, who is attributed with leading the largest mass movement in black history. The Pan-Africanist leader formed the first Universal Negro Improvement Association and African Communities League (UNIA-ACL) division in Harlem, New York. At its height, the UNIA had more than one thousand chapters across the world with over one million members. Garvey's weekly newspaper, *Negro World,* was established in New York City.[6] It was an attempt to convey his message of freedom to black people. During the 1920s, Garvey's UNIA-ACL, according to historian Lawrence W. Levine, was "the broadest mass movement" in African American history.[7]

Leaders like Booker T. Washington and W. E. B. Du Bois emerged also during this time as founders and activists of organizations like the Universal Negro Improvement Association (UNIA), Niagara Movement, the NAACP, and the National League on Urban Conditions among Negroes (now the National Urban League). It is important to note that while there were many intellectual leaders during the Harlem Renaissance, for others, leadership was a decision. Garvey pointed out the lack of African American leadership and vowed to help develop leaders. He said, "'Where is the black man's Government?' 'Where is his King and his kingdom?' 'Where is his President, his country, and his ambassador, his army, his navy, his men of big affairs?' I could not find them, and then I declared, 'I will help to make them.'"[8] Perhaps, Josey, like Garvey, born of Jamaican stock, had a spark that would burgeon to revolutionize a generation of librarians.

The quest for Josey and the formative influences of his development can be traced back to this history of inhumane treatment of African Americans. He was born in an era where blacks made significant progress, yet there was still much to be done. Like those who paved the way before him, he too became a visionary, and a leader against inequality. Blacks collaborated with organizations to neutralize the state of oppression of African Americans, resulting in the Niagara Movement. Many of the great Harlem Renaissance icons, such as Du Bois, Garvey, Alain Locke, and Langston Hughes, were role models for Josey. Regina Anderson Andrews, the first African American librarian to head a branch of the New York Public Library, was a key member of the Harlem Renaissance. She cohosted a salon and was an active participant in the little theater movement as both an actress and playwright.[9]

GROWING UP IN PORTSMOUTH

It was clear from the beginning, at least among those who knew Josey during his formative years, that he was a unique individual who possessed outstanding qualities that set him apart from many of his peers. As a child he was inquisitive, feisty, and a visionary.[10] Although his path to prominence was often bumpy, he always maintained optimism and faith even in the direst of circumstances. Josey never let the dehumanizing experiences of racism and poverty deter him from achieving his goals. He said that he became an "'incredible dreamer with a tiny spark hidden somewhere inside you, which cannot die, even which you cannot kill or quench and which tortures you horribly because all the odds are against its continual burning.'"[11] This quote by Josey was inspired by Eldridge Cleaver's classic biography, *Soul on Ice*.[12] In an autobiographical chapter in *The Black Librarian in America*, Josey quoted the following passage by Cleaver as being descriptive of his own quest to be a man and not a second-class citizen:

> And why does it make you sad to see how everything hangs by such thin and whimsical threads? Because you're a dreamer, an incredible dreamer with a tiny spark hidden somewhere inside you which cannot die, even which you cannot kill or quench and which tortures you horribly because all the odds are against its continual burning. In the midst of the foulest decay and putrid savagery, this spark speaks to you of beauty, of human warmth and kindness, of goodness, of greatness, of heroism, of martyrdom, and it speaks to you of love.[13]

On January 20, 1924, in Norfolk, Virginia, Elonnie Junius (E. J.) was born to parents Willie and Frances (Bailey) Josey. Although the 1930 census lists Josey's mother as Fannie, she was commonly referred to by family and friends as Frances.[14] Like many residents of Portsmouth, Willie and Frances had lived in North Carolina and migrated to Virginia after WWI to take advantage of the burgeoning economy. Frances completed a normal teacher-training school and taught for one year in North Carolina before marrying Willie.[15] Normal school offered students two years of training beyond high school. It was common for African Americans to attend normal school to become teachers because few blacks were able to afford expenses for a college or university education. Many African Americans chose teaching as a career because it was one of the few highly respected professions.

Willie Josey served in one of the battalions during WWI. Upon being discharged from the military, he made a living working at the Norfolk Naval Shipyard in Portsmouth as a laborer. Josey remembers his father as being hardworking and full of pride: "He could neither read nor write but, coming from good Jamaican stock, he was a proud man who often carried a paper under his arm in order to give the impression that he was educated."[16]

Shortly after Josey's birth, his parents moved five miles west of the Elizabeth River to the city of Portsmouth. Historic Portsmouth has a rich past that provides context in understanding Josey's early life. It was established as a town by act of the General Assembly of Virginia in 1752 and as a city in 1858.[17] However, the formation and development of Portsmouth as a munici-pality can be traced back to a much earlier period when the Hampton Roads region was first settled as a plantation community. In 1608, twelve English explorers, led by Captain John Smith, traveled up the Chesapeake River

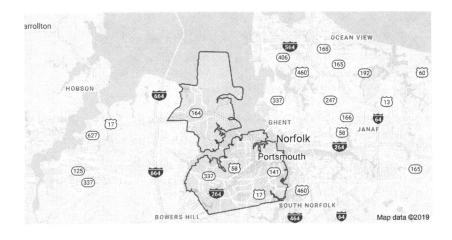

Figure 2.1.   Map of Hampton Roads region. *Google Maps*

(known today as the Elizabeth River) and stumbled on a spacious land they envisioned as a perfect location for shipbuilding and commercial use. However, it took more than two hundred years before that dream became reality. In 1752, Lieutenant Colonel William Crawford, a wealthy merchant and shipowner, was granted the land and annexed the town from his extensive landholdings. He surveyed the property and named it after the great naval "port" and dockyard in England.[18]

What came to be known as the Gosport Naval Yard yielded ample opportunities for individuals with small businesses to obtain inexpensive labor.[19] Consequently, there was an influx of people who migrated to the city to take advantage of the opportunity to make money. Similarly, businessmen who wanted to capitalize on the thriving market and opportunities to make lucrative deals relocated to Portsmouth. For example, "Scottish merchants who operated ship stores across the river in Norfolk relocated to Portsmouth in the early 1750s. This newly established town gave these merchants more land on which to build their wharves and warehouses and more opportunity to dominate the industry in that town."[20]

The emergence of a small number of African and later African American populations, most of whom were enslaved, came from local plantations and lived in town for convenience. "In 1860 Portsmouth was a city of 9,500 persons of whom about one-third were Negroes."[21] The shipping industry that was based primarily on riverboat trading in the interior, the ferry service between Norfolk and Portsmouth, and the port commerce, provided an abundance of jobs for enslaved African Americans. The seventeenth through nineteenth centuries were especially hard for blacks living in Portsmouth. Slavery was the single defining institution that dominated life for them, and, even if they were free on bond, segregation laws made it challenging for blacks to make progress. Segregation made life very difficult for free blacks. They struggled with employment discrimination, job displacement from white immigrants, and exclusion from enjoying the privileges of society.

The twentieth century gave way to Jim Crow as the heart of American life. The economic and political achievements of blacks in the post-WWI era were replaced by a heightened sense of discrimination which fostered in systemic racism. Jim Crow laws continued the violence that occurred in the nineteenth century, making blacks' pursuit for equality unattainable. Thousands of lynchings, rape, and intimidation tactics were common practice under Jim Crow. Emmett Till, a fourteen-year-old African American boy, was lynched in Mississippi in 1955 after a white woman said she was offended by him in her family's grocery store. The brutality of his murder and the fact that his killers were acquitted drew attention to the long history of violent persecution of African Americans in the United States. Till posthumously became an icon of the civil rights movement.

While segregation was nothing new, the hope for equality began fading as it became increasingly obvious that white America would not allow blacks to integrate and incorporate into mainstream America. The economic boom of the twenties was short-lived. By the time Josey was five years old, a dramatic global economic downturn occurred, and the United States was on the brink of financial disaster. The world in which Josey and his four younger siblings (Robert, Loyd, Melba, and Edward) spent their early years was a stranger to the democracy that President Woodrow Wilson vowed to defend when he announced the entry of the United States into WWI. Segregation reigned in Virginia and elsewhere in the Deep South. Slavery may have been outlawed after the North won the Civil War, but across the South, many blacks lived in virtual slavery as sharecroppers on farms owned by whites. Blacks were blamed for the Civil War and the loss of the "Southern way of life" when the Confederacy was vanquished, and blacks were separated from whites in almost every area of life. By law, the Josey children had to play in separate areas of public parks, drink from public fountains marked "colored," and sit in separate cars or sections designated for blacks.

Financial hardship intensified the social climate in Portsmouth. The stock market crash on October 29, 1929, was the final blow to an already sluggish economy and ultimately sent the United States into the Great Depression. The Great Depression of the 1930s reduced industrial employment and the flow of black migrants to the North. Despite that fact, 458,000 more blacks left the South than moved in. Many of them were sharecroppers and other tenant farmers displaced by New Deal crop-reduction programs.[22] The population of Portsmouth declined significantly because of the Depression. According to the 1920 census, the population of Portsmouth was 54,387; the population reported for the 1930 census was 45,704.[23]

MOUNT HERMON

The Depression was especially difficult for African Americans living in Portsmouth. The Josey family resided in a small urban, impoverished community in the Mount Hermon section of the city. This community was developed in 1898 by a New Jersey native who moved to the area from South Hampton County; he built up the neighborhood courtesy of a $10,000 loan from a wealthy Portsmouth judge.[24] The first house was built on the corner of Glasgow Street and Florida Avenue. Ironically, the house in which Josey was raised, 1136 Florida Avenue, between Queen and Glasgow Streets, was on the same block. Although the property is now demolished due to redevelopment, an examination of the 1930 Portsmouth Sanborn map[25] indicates that the home was a midsized, single-family dwelling located near the end of the block.

Many residents of Mount Hermon were strong community leaders and teachers who had a great influence on the children who lived there. They provided a strong sense of self-worth. Moses Gibson, a former resident of Mount Hermon in the 1930s and schoolmate of Josey, recalls that Mount Hermon was a community of "struggling people." Although many residents owned their homes, many members of the community did not have jobs. Those who did worked at the railroad or the naval yard. Many of the Mount Hermon residents believed that the neighborhood possessed a real sense of community during the 1930s and 1940s. Parents always stressed the importance of education, and, despite the expense, they tried to get their children into college.[26] Gibson remembers Josey as being "very smart" and "studious." Similarly, his sister, Rachel Gibson, who resided in Los Angeles, also recalled Josey as being very studious and quiet.[27]

The church played a major role in the lives of residents in Portsmouth, particularly in Mount Hermon. Since the nineteenth century, the growth of the Protestant religion among African Americans gave birth to what came to be known as the "black church" in the United States. From the white Baptist and Methodist missionaries sent to convert enslaved Africans, to the earliest pioneers of the independent black denominations, to the fluent rhetoric of Du

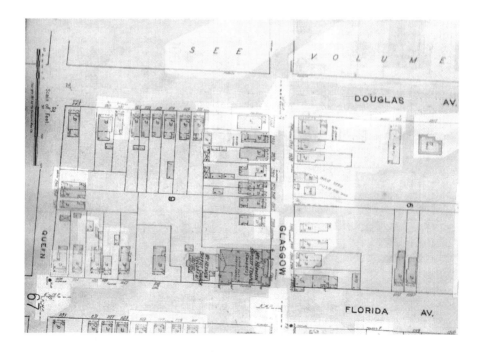

Figure 2.2. Map of Mount Hermon neighborhood. *Courtesy of Portsmouth Public Library*

Bois, the story of the black church is an account of struggle during constant racism and oppression. It is also a story of constant change, and cultural cohesion among enslaved African Americans in their communities. In Portsmouth, the black church has served as a breeding ground for black political activism, as well as a social meeting place, ever since post–Civil War days when blacks had their separate churches in which to worship but were barred from meeting in other public places.[28] During segregation, the church became an indispensable institution for the residents of Portsmouth. Authors Cassandra Newby-Alexander and Mae Breckenridge-Haywood contend that "it was through the black church, especially in this post-war era, that literary and benevolent organizations and self-help groups emerged as agencies for the improvement of the social and moral conditions of African Americans."[29] From the Emanuel African Methodist Episcopal Church (one of the oldest and largest churches in Portsmouth) to the Mount Hermon Baptist Temple (that established the first Boy Scout troop in Portsmouth), the black church provided a solid foundation for spiritual and personal development.

The church had an integral role in Josey's life. His family attended the second largest Baptist church in Mount Hermon, Celestial Baptist Church. It was at Celestial where Josey found his love of God and music. Josey's daughter, Amina Jacqueline Turner, describes Josey as religious with a strong faith in God. She further asserts that his favorite scripture was Philippians 4:13; "I can do all things through Christ who strengthens me." He enjoyed gospel and classical music and eventually went on to play the organ at neighborhood churches to earn money for his family. Josey took private piano and organ lessons from several outstanding teachers from the Tidewater region. He was especially grateful to Elnora Wright, who tutored him during his high school years and provided him with the seeds of musical training, even when he had no money to afford the lessons.[30] Josey continued his membership at Celestial long after he moved away from the city and would often visit whenever he was in town. Former pastor, Reverend Leon Boone, recalls how Josey would wave to him from the back of the church when he came to Portsmouth.[31] Fellow parishioner, Marian King, remembers how he would "faithfully send $100 a month to the church as part of his tithe and offering. I think that speaks to the kind of person he is."[32]

Josey and his siblings attended segregated Mount Hermon Elementary School (grades 1–7). The school was in the downtown area and experienced great overcrowding during the 1930s. According to the superintendent's report, Mount Hermon Elementary School was an eight-room building with fourteen teachers. To accommodate the overflow of students, they rented two additional dilapidated rooms at a nearby Masonic Temple, where students could only attend school part-time.[33] There was also an excess of students at I. C. Norcom High School, where Josey completed his secondary education.

The only high school available to African Americans in Portsmouth during the 1930s and 1940s, I. C. Norcom High School was named after distinguished educator, Israel C. Norcom, who migrated to Portsmouth after graduating from Harvard and Yale Universities. Norcom served as the principal at the Chestnut Street Colored School; three years after his death in 1937, the school was named in his honor. It was at Norcom where Josey excelled academically. Many of his schoolmates remember Josey as being very intelligent with leader-like qualities.[34] For example, he was always interested in reading and learning, and he encouraged his siblings, as well as his fellow classmates, to also excel in their studies. Josey also took a leading role in his chorus group. Not only did he sing, but on some occasions, he also directed the choir.[35] Josey credits his dedicated elementary and high school teachers for providing a good educational background even though black Portsmouth schools did not have all the facilities that the white schools did. "The teachers wanted to give us more; they must have believed that we were going to outlive segregation and that someday we were going to be called upon to compete in a multicultural world."[36]

Josey attributes his mother for "fostering and nurturing the desire for knowledge, wisdom, and achievement."[37] He recalls his mother reading sto-

Figure 2.3. I. C. Norcom High School, 1920. *I. C. Norcom High School*

ries to them, insisting that they read at least one extra book in addition to their school work each week and making them memorize poetry that she had learned at the private Presbyterian school she attended when she was growing up. He also remembers participating in school and church cultural activities. Although he was raised in poverty, often without enough food or adequate clothing, his mother encouraged the Josey children to pursue their creative talents. Consequently, he and his siblings never felt poor:

> The reason we did not feel poor was because my mother gave us a lot of cultural enrichment. She taught us all kinds of music, all kinds of poems, and we did not have a radio or television, so we would sing these songs and we would try to recite the poetry and do dramatics. I think it also helped us, all of the children to excel in school because we were doing things outside of school that our teachers had not asked us to do and yet they were beneficial to our growth and development, culturally and educationally. [38]

Unfortunately, Josey and many of his classmates did not have the luxury of using the Portsmouth Public Library while growing up in Mount Hermon. African Americans could not use the "whites only" public library in the city. The only library blacks were permitted to use was the segregated Portsmouth Community Library, which was housed in the Parish House of St. James Episcopal Church near I. C. Norcom High School. Josey recalled that "the only library I used in my hometown was the segregated high-school library presided over by a fine former English teacher, Mrs. Margaret Bond Jackson." [39] The library was open from 1937 to 1941 and was ultimately closed due to lack of funding. It was not until several years later that another library was built for African Americans. The Portsmouth Colored Community Library opened its doors in 1945 and was in the heart of Portsmouth on South Street near Effingham. This small, one-story brick building was purchased with donations made by Portsmouth's black and white citizens and subsidized by the city. With the rise of the civil rights movement in the 1960s, and the integration of blacks in the larger community, there no longer was a need for a separate library. The Portsmouth Colored Community Library closed its doors in 1963 but is currently a museum dedicated to the history of African Americans in Portsmouth.

Given Josey's experiences while growing up in a segregated town, it is remarkable that he would be placed in the "the company of the great leaders in the history of American librarianship." [40] Some would argue that Josey had an even bigger impact on international librarianship. [41] Nevertheless, Josey rose from these humble beginnings to the top of his profession.

Adult responsibilities came early for young Josey. His father passed away unexpectedly while he was a sophomore in high school. As the eldest of five children, he had to help support his family. The following year, he graduated early so that he could find employment. He took on a number of jobs, such as

Figure 2.4.   Portsmouth Community Library. *Courtesy of Portsmouth Public Library*

dishwasher, porter, and stock clerk. He also played the organ and piano at churches in the neighborhood until he was drafted in the army to serve in WWII.[42]

ARMY YEARS

World War II blasted its way onto the American scene on the infamous morning of December 7, 1941, when Japanese fighters flew over Pearl Harbor and rained a hail of bombs and bullets on the slumbering US naval base. In 1940, with the war raging in Europe, the US federal government was doing all it could to prepare for eventual participation, including training men to fight in various branches of the military. After the United States declared war on Germany and Japan, a new selective service act required all men ages 18–45 to register for the military draft.

Josey was drafted into the army on May 18, 1943,[43] and was stationed in the Deep South, where he was part of the segregated units. The structure of the military did not permit blacks to serve in combat roles. The African American community in the United States embarked on a "Double V" campaign: victory over enemies on the battlefields abroad and victory over dis-

Figure 2.5.   E. J. Josey pictured (upper left) with I. C. Norcom High School classmates.

crimination at home. The Double V Campaign was an effort during WWII that crusaded for full citizenship rights for African Americans fighting for the United States in the war. It was organized by the *Pittsburgh Courier*, one of the most prominent African American newspapers of the time, and was a weekly feature of the newspaper for more than a year. The primary objectives of the campaign were to increase knowledge about the many African Americans who were overseas fighting for their country and to petition for them to be given full citizenship rights when they finally returned home.[44]

The campaign also sought to garner support for the African American community by publishing articles, editorials, and letters in the *Courier*. The editor believed that by showing support and encouraging the black community to do all it could for the war effort, they could in turn help convince the US government to do all it could to increase racial equality in the country. This idea quickly gained the backing of numerous other African American newspapers and soon grew into a national effort. Unfortunately, for Josey, life in the military did not offer much cover from overt racism. Assigned to an all-black squadron, Josey served as assistant to several chaplains and played the organ for religious services. He experienced two significant events that had a lasting impression on his life. First, it was in the army that he had the opportunity to use his first nonsegregated library. Josey recalls how pleased he was when he learned of his access to reading materials in the military, which he regarded as one of the greatest benefits of serving in the armed forces during this time. "The opportunity to read a wide variety of materials in the Army caused me to continue my quest for knowledge and revived my desire for a college education."[45] He also had an encounter with overt racism that permanently changed his life:

> As I stood in line with hundreds of other soldiers waiting to board the local bus, the bus driver, in savage tones said, "Boy, step back and let the white soldiers get on first." I refused to get out of the line and, in a bewildered and halting voice, said I was a soldier serving my country and had a right to board the bus in my turn. The white bus driver was infuriated and pulled a revolver, but in spite of his "putrid savagery," I refused to move, and he shoved me out of line. After this act, which could even have resulted in my death, I became an implacable foe of segregation and second class citizenship.[46]

Just like many of Josey's childhood experiences, his time in the military helped shape his leadership and activism later in life. When he left the army, he held true to his words to never buckle to discrimination and to be a fighter of segregation.

COLLEGE YEARS AND GRADUATE SCHOOL

In 1947, Josey enrolled at Howard University in Washington, DC, where he was admitted to the school of music. He later transferred to the College of Liberal Arts after his second quarter because he did not want to invest five years of coursework studying music. He changed his major to history and completed his undergraduate degree in three years. He decided to pursue teaching as a career stemming from the admiration of his mother and his upbringing in Portsmouth where teachers were the main professionals with whom young blacks were best acquainted in their community.[47]

Howard University was commissioned as a university by an act of the US Congress in 1867. It remains the only historically black college and university (HBCU) to hold this distinction.[48] It was originally conceived as a theological school and was later labeled "the capstone of Negro education" because of its central role in the African American educational experience.[49] Perhaps it was the series of racial incidents in Josey's early life that led him to attend an HBCU—a place where he did not have be concerned with discrimination and where he would have the space to develop his leadership and excel in his studies.

After several unsuccessful attempts at obtaining a teaching position in history, he took a job as a desk assistant in the Journalism Library at Columbia University while working on his master's degree in history. From 1950 to 1952, he worked in several of the departmental libraries at Columbia and was encouraged to pursue librarianship as a career by his supervisor, Basil Miller. In 1952, Josey left Columbia and went to work at the New York State Library and subsequently entered the State University of New York (SUNY) Library School. With the assistance of a scholarship from the New York Library Association and a part-time job at the New York State Library, he was able to afford a second master's degree. [50]

Josey's first year in library school was quite challenging. Unlike his graduate experience at Columbia, he was the only black student in the program. Augusta Baker, a distinguished children's librarian, was a graduate of the program twenty years earlier, but for the most part African Americans were not enrolled in the Albany program. [51] Josey remembers his experience with his classmates as a positive one:

> Most of my classmates were understanding and, like most library school students of that day, they were anxiously looking forward to graduation. My library school class produced several outstanding librarians. Two are now directors of New York State Public Library Systems, one serves on the Board of Regents Advisory Council on Libraries, two are consultants with state agencies, and one is a professor in one of the major library schools in the country. [52]

A recurring theme throughout Josey's life was that he was in the company of individuals who were successful. His sister, after leaving the armed forces, went on to be a distinguished teacher in Texas. One of his closest childhood friends, Charles E. Gray, a retired school administrator and later a faculty member at Virginia State College, coauthored *Above the Storm*, a book detailing the historic account of the student walkout of the R. R. Moton High School in Prince Edward County, Virginia. [53] This walkout resulted in *Davis v. County School Board*, [54] one of the cases that led to the 1954 Supreme Court decision outlawing segregation in public schools. Several graduates from I. C. Norcom High School went on to doctoral study, including Willard Stanback, former associate professor of mathematics and statistics at Norfolk State University, and Dr. James Eaton, former professor emeritus of English at Savannah State College, who is listed in the *2000–2002 Who's Who in America*. In 1987, Josey was recognized by the city of Portsmouth as a national notable. This honor placed him in the company of jazz great Ruth Brown and Carl M. Brashear, the first black US Navy diver, portrayed by Cuba Gooding Jr. in the 2000 film *Men of Honor*.

It was not uncommon for a faction of blacks to be considered the professional elite within their communities, and Portsmouth was no exception. In keeping with the philosophy of Ida B. Wells, who insisted that the African American community must win justice through its own efforts, several blacks in Portsmouth rose to prominence by struggling against racial oppression. Authors Newby-Alexander and Breckenridge-Haywood contend that between 1900 and 1960, African Americans in Portsmouth formed a network of "middle class" professionals to counteract the practices of segregation and exclusion.[55] Efforts from individuals like educator Norcom; Jeffrey T. Wilson, an African American writer who wrote the column *Colored Notes* for the city's newspaper; Dr. Helen Mewborn-Watts, who was the first black female physician in Portsmouth; and countless others were "the fraternal, political, and financial models for blacks in and around Portsmouth."[56] This close-knit, insulated community allowed African Americans to sustain themselves during the days of Jim Crow. From this community, Josey emerged as a leader in the fight for civil rights.

Josey was a dreamer who not only wanted a better life for his family, but he wanted a better America. He wanted a society that was fair and equal for everyone. It was the impetus for the spark that he would bring to a generation of library professionals.

NOTES

1. Chad Williams, "African Americans and World War I," African and African Diasporan Transformations in the 20th Century, accessed May 22, 2018, http://exhibitions.nypl.org/africanaage/essay-world-war-i.html.

2. Jim Crow laws were a series of racist measures enacted from 1876 to 1964 that discriminated against African Americans. The effects of these laws are still prevalent today.

3. Ethelene Whitmire, "Breaking the Color Barrier: Regina Andrews and the New York Public Library," *Libraries and the Cultural Record* 42, no. 4 (2007): 411, doi:10.1353/lac2007.0068.

4. A movement coined by philosopher Alain Locke that refers to the transformation of African Americans by ridding themselves of all racial and social impediments that obstructed black achievement.

5. Jennifer Latson, "How America's First Self-Made Female Millionaire Built Her Fortune," *Time*, December 24, 2014, http://time.com/3641122/sarah-breedlove-walker/.

6. Lawrence W. Levine, *The Unpredictable Past: Explorations in American Cultural History* (New York: Oxford University Press, 1993), 121.

7. Levine, *Unpredictable Past*, 122.

8. "The Philosophy and Opinions of Marcus Garvey, or, Africa for the Africans," in *Philosophy and Opinions of Marcus Garvey*, ed. Amy Jacques-Garvey, with an introduction by Robert A. Hill (New York: Atheneum, 1992), first published 1923–1925 by Amy Jacques-Garvey, 126.

9. Ethelene Whitmire, *Regina Anderson Andrews: Harlem Renaissance Librarian* (Urbana: University of Illinois Press, 2014), 32–47, 61–74.

10. Willard Stanback, personal interview with the author, December 11, 2007.

11. E. J. Josey, "A Dreamer—with a Tiny Spark," in *The Black Librarian in America*, ed. E. J. Josey (Metuchen, NJ: Scarecrow Press, 1970), 298.

12. Eldridge Cleaver, *Soul on Ice* (New York: Dell Publishing Co., 1968).

13. Josey, "A Dreamer," 297.

14. United States Census Bureau, "1930 United States Census Population Statistics," accessed November 9, 2007, http://search.ancestrylibrary.com/cgi-bin.sse.dll?db=1930usfedcen.

15. E. J. Josey, personal interview with the author, April 8, 2007.

16. Josey, "Dreamer," 298.

17. Marshall W. Butt, *Portsmouth under Four Flags: 1752–1961* (Portsmouth, VA: Portsmouth Historical Association, 1961), 1, 3, 20.

18. Cassandra Newby-Alexander, Mae Breckenridge-Haywood, and African American Historical Society of Portsmouth, *Black America Series: Portsmouth Virginia* (Charleston, SC: Arcadia Publishing, 2003), 7.

19. Newby-Alexander, *Portsmouth Virginia*, 27.

20. Newby-Alexander, *Portsmouth Virginia*, 7.

21. Butt, *Portsmouth under Four Flags*, 20.

22. United States Bureau of the Census, *Historical Statistics of the United States, Colonial Times to 1957* (Washington, DC, 1960), https://www.census.gov/library/publications/1960/compendia/hist_stats_colonial-1957.html.

23. "Number of Inhabitants–Virginia," in United States Bureau of the Census, *Census of Population: 1960*, vol. 1, *Characteristics of the Population*, pt. 48, *Virginia* (Washington, DC: Government Printing Office, 1963), 11, https://www2.census.gov/prod2/decennial/documents/09768066v1p48ch2.pdf.

24. Mount Hermon Reunion, *Fighting Spirit Forever 1990* (Portsmouth, VA: Mount Hermon Souvenir Journal Committee, 1990).

25. Sanborn Maps illustrate the commercial and residential sections of a city.

26. Moses Gibson, in personal communication with the author, November 21, 2007.

27. Rachel Gibson, in personal communication with the author, November 24, 2007.

28. M. Adrine, "Churches Traditionally Forums for Blacks," *Currents* (February 16, 1986): 4.

29. Newby-Alexander, *Portsmouth Virginia*, 10.

30. Josey, "Dreamer," 298.

31. Leon Boone, personal interview with the author, December 11, 2007.

32. Marian King, in personal communication with the author, December 12, 2007.

33. *Annual Reports of the Public Schools of Portsmouth, Virginia: School Years 1924–1925 to 1936–1937* (Portsmouth, VA: National Printing Co., 1980).

34. James Eaton, personal interview with the author, December 14, 2007; Willard Stanback, personal interview with the author, November 23, 2007; Ann. Stancil, personal interview with the author, December 1, 2007; Mary Todd, personal interview with the author, December 9, 2007.

35. Stanback, in personal communication with the author, November 23, 2007.

36. E. J. Josey, in personal communication with the author, March 29, 2001.

37. Josey, "Dreamer," 298.

38. E. J. Josey, in personal communication with the author, February 14, 2001.

39. E. J. Josey, in personal communication with the author, March 10, 2001.

40. Clara Stanton Jones, "E. J. Josey: Librarian for All Seasons," in *E. J. Josey: An Activist Librarian*, ed. Ismail Abdullahi (Metuchen, NJ: Scarecrow Press, 1992), 1.

41. Al Kagan, personal interview with the author, April 9, 2007; *see* Vivian Davidson Hewitt, "An Internationalist in ALA and IFLA," in *E. J. Josey: An Activist Librarian*, ed. Ismail Abdullahi (Metuchen, NJ: Scarecrow Press, 1992), 181–93.

42. Josey, in personal communication with the author, February 14, 2001.

43. National Archives and Records Administration, "United States World War II Army Enlistment Records, 1938–1946," in *FamilySearch*, accessed April 12, 2010, https://familysearch.org/search/collection/results?count=20&query=%2Bgivenname%3AElonnie~%20%   2Bsurname%3AJosey~%20%2Brace%3ABlack& collection_id=2028680.

44. Rawn James, *The Double V: How Wars, Protest, and Harry Truman Desegregated America's Military* (New York: Bloomsbury Press, 2013), 137–43.

45. E. J. Josey, personal interview with the author, April 10, 2007.

46. Josey, "Dreamer," 299–300.

47. Josey, "Dreamer," 300.

48. Alonzo Smith, "Howard University (1867–)," BlackPast, February 8, 2010, http://www.blackpast.org/aah/howard-university-1867.

49. Smith, "Howard University."

50. Josey, "Dreamer," 300.

51. Josey, "Dreamer," 301.

52. Josey, "Dreamer," 301.

53. Charles E. Gray and John Arthur Stokes, *Above the Storm* (Hampton, VA: Four-G Publishers, 2004).

54. Davis v. City School Board, 103 F. Supp. 337 (E.D. Va. 1952), *rev'd sub nom.* Brown v. Board of Education, 349 U.S. 294 (1955).

55. Newby-Alexander, *Portsmouth Virginia*, 8.

56. Newby-Alexander, *Portsmouth Virginia*, 8.

Chapter Three

Early Years

The Transformation Begins

Brown v. Board of Education was decided in 1954. It was the year before Josey graduated from the library science program at SUNY. In the *Brown* decision, the Supreme Court ruled that separation of school children "generates a feeling of inferiority as to their status in the community that may affect their hearts and minds in a way unlikely ever to be undone."[1] Even after the court ordered that school segregation be dismantled, many city and state officials ignored the ruling and refused to integrate their schools. The federal government tried to enforce the law, but some communities resisted. Battles over school desegregation raged across the South throughout the 1950s and many have argued that segregation of public schools did not officially end until the Civil Rights Act of 1964.[2] Southern public libraries were segregated and experienced their own share of turmoil during the era of Jim Crow. Young black community activists were instrumental in leading protests, sit-ins, and challenges to the court to fight for access to library materials and services.[3] It was early in Josey's professional career that we see the genesis of transformative leadership. One tenet of the framework conceptualized by Bass—*idealized influence*—or the degree to which leaders act in admirable ways that causes followers to identify with them—can be seen during his directorships at Delaware State College and Savannah State College libraries.

Brown was a crucial juncture in the civil rights movement. It helped establish the precedent that "separate-but-equal" adopted in *Plessy v. Ferguson*[4] was not, in fact, equal at all. It illuminated the deep racial divides that persisted in education and in public spaces. For Josey to thrive in this era was nothing short of extraordinary. He received an undergraduate degree and two

Figure 3.1. Miles College student speaking to librarians during the sit-in at the Birmingham Public Library, 1963. *Courtesy of Alabama Department of Archives and History. Donated by Alabama Media Group. Unknown photographer,* **Birmingham News**

master's degrees in a hostile climate of racial intolerance. Even more astonishing is that he pursued a career that was not always welcoming to African Americans despite many who were attracted to librarianship long before its professionalization. Richard T. Greener, the first African American graduate of Harvard University, who in addition to teaching philosophy, Latin, and Greek at the University of South Carolina, was a librarian and helped reorganize the library's collection when it was left disorderly after the Civil War in 1875, a year before the founding of the ALA. Edward Christopher Williams, the first black American to graduate from a library science program, entered the profession twenty years later in 1896.[5] While many blacks gravitated to the profession, they would continue to struggle for equal rights well into the twenty-first century. Today, African Americans make up approximately 14,250 of 190,000 librarians in the United States.[6]

Library and information science students are generally eager and excited to enter the profession after completing their degree—Josey was no exception. In fact, while in library school, he took advantage of many opportunities to increase his chances for landing a librarian's position. He worked in the New York State Library and visited several libraries to network with professional librarians.

PHILADELPHIA FREE PUBLIC LIBRARY

Colloquially referred to as the "city of brotherly love," Philadelphia was one of the first American cities that promoted the ideals of liberty and freedom. Known for its role in the American Revolutionary War, this industrial metropolis in the United States also convened the Continental Congress and was the site for the signing of the Declaration of Independence.

In the nineteenth century, Philadelphia was at the center of the abolitionist movement and had the largest free black population in the United States. African Americans gravitated to the city during the civil rights movement, and its black population has gradually increased ever since. Philadelphia has one of the largest African American populations in the country. The migration of blacks to Philadelphia in the 1950s and 1960s may have been a factor in Josey's decision to begin his career in librarianship.

The Free Library of Philadelphia (FLP) opened its doors in 1894 as "a general library which shall be free to all," thanks to a bequest of $225,000 from a relative of the provost of the University of Pennsylvania.[7] Multiple branches, including a new central branch, were added in 1903, courtesy of a donation of $1.5 million dollars by philanthropist Andrew Carnegie.[8] Carnegie ultimately gave away $60 million to fund a system of 1,689 public libraries across the country.[9] His gift to FLP facilitated and ultimately ensured the expansion of the library through many moves and renovations. "On June 2, 1927, the massive Central Library opened for service at its present location on Logan Square."[10] The building was "in the planning stages since 1911; however, various obstacles, including World War I, halted progress on the building."[11] Today, it "serves as the main library and administrative headquarters for the Free Library of Philadelphia system."[12]

The year 1951 was landmark in Philadelphia, particularly on the political scene. In April, voters approved a charter that would transform the city's patronage-laden government. This new charter increased the powers of the mayor and shifted control over most of municipal jobs, which had previously been appointed positions. Because of the new charter, Philadelphia was the first city in the nation to include a ban on racial and religious discrimination in city employment and services. In November of that year, a Democratic mayor was voted in for the first time in the twentieth century; the election also mandated the protection of civil rights of all Philadelphians.[13] The liberal milieu of Philadelphia attracted countless African Americans to the city

Figure 3.2.   Free Library of Philadelphia, 1927. *Courtesy of Free Library of Philadelphia Special Collections*

during the heightened epoch of unrest in the country. This may have been one of the reasons Josey was drawn to the city.

Josey was excited to begin his career as a professional librarian at the FLP. He and fellow classmate Murray Bob, who would eventually become the director of the public library system in Jamestown, New York, joined the staff following graduation from the State University of New York Library School in 1953.[14] They were recruited by the highly respected librarian Emerson Greenaway.[15] Greenaway is probably best known for designing what was called the "Greenaway Plan." Libraries would tell vendors and wholesalers what type of subject areas they were interested in and indicate books published in that subject area. Vendors and wholesalers would then mail books to the library for examination and purchase. If libraries did not like a book, they would return it.[16] Under Greenaway's leadership, the Philadelphia library implemented programs such as these and did very well. However, Greenaway was overwhelmed by significant challenges. One of the problems he inherited was that the FLP recently implemented the civil service requirement. This regulation mandated that all new employees be hired based on merit, using a competitive examination. When Josey and Bob were hired, they both passed the exam; however, a grandfather clause protected the librarians who were currently employed by granting them civil service status. Most of these individuals received their credentials by attending library training classes that were offered by the library.[17] According to Josey, these "'untrained' librarians" resented him and his friend Bob, which created great dissension among the employees.[18]

Greenaway's first initiative was to organize the Central Library into subject departments. It was decided that the subject areas would be staffed by specialists. Since Josey had a master's degree in history, he wanted a position in the social science section, but despite his desire and qualifications, it was decided that he would be sent to a branch library. Josey immediately protested and sought the help of his minister, Reverend Leon Sullivan, who was active in the civil rights movement, to mediate on his behalf and was able to convince the library to give Josey the position. However, this made matters worse for him. Often, he was reduced to performing clerical tasks that hardly required a master's degree in library science, and Josey became outspoken about what he perceived to be injustice.[19]

Moreover, while working in the reference department, Josey was often sought out to answer patrons' questions that his colleagues could not answer. This presented more problems for the neophyte librarian. Although he did not have a great deal of experience working in libraries, he relied on the knowledge he had from his library science program, as well as the experience from working at the New York Public Library, which made him far more advanced than those who had been working in the library for some time. This situation was further complicated when Josey was the first African American librarian to work at the FLP. The hostility of the staff made it unbearable for him, and he became disappointed with librarianship and decided to leave the profession completely. Interestingly, the notion of "brotherly love" that Philadelphia is historically known for eluded Josey and propelled him to leave librarianship to pursue teaching. He describes in detail his disappointment and dismay about his first professional position at the FLP:

> The year at Philadelphia was one of frustration, for Murray and I were both doing clerical routines which certainly did not require matriculation from a library school. To compound the situation, before the coming of the Greenaway era and the new democratic administration, the Republican ward leaders had influenced the library administration to appoint high school graduates from their wards as librarians. With the establishment of Civil Service, this practice ceased. There was a grandfather clause that protected these "untrained" librarians, and they were given Civil Service status as librarians; however, they resented the library school graduates that Greenaway was recruiting, and, of course, there was additional resentment toward [Josey because he] was black.[20]

Despite his unpleasant experience at the FLP, Josey respected Greenaway for his honesty and abilities as a director and was greatly influenced by his first public library director. Josey believed that it was middle management and the non-library-school-trained personnel that perpetuated racism in his first professional position and not Greenaway, who he remained friends with until his retirement from librarianship. The threat of library workers, who had an advanced degree, may also have been a factor that led to the hostile environment. Nevertheless, Josey decided he could no longer stay at the FLP and accepted a position as an instructor in the social sciences at Savannah State College.[21] Friend Clara Stanton Jones recalls Josey's experience:

> During the Greenaway tenure, the Library would flourish, but it had been beset by grave problems before he was able to effect a transformation. Among many other things, in the confusing maze of troubles, racism was blatant. E. J. stood it for one year and then accepted a position as History Instructor at Savannah State College in Georgia. However, in his very brief stint at Philadelphia, he gained great respect for Greenaway's integrity and capability, and they remained friends. E. J. says he believes his report of serious frustrations did not get past the old entrenched middle management.[22]

Following Josey's tumultuous year at the FLP, he would go on to spend the next twelve years of his career working at HBCUs. First, he worked as a history instructor at Savannah State College, then at Delaware State College Library, and then back to Savannah State College Library.[23]

HBCUs were created in the mid-1860s as institutions intended to serve the African American community. They often provided a place for blacks to grow and develop leadership skills during segregation. For many, it was an opportunity to share experiences and obtain mutual support from other African Americans. This notion was also theorized by Earl Lewis, who studied African American life in Norfolk, Virginia, by examining the lives of people after "they moved to the city—the jobs they obtained, the assistance they secured, the houses they lived in, the families they built, the battles they waged, the victories they realized, the defeats they suffered, the institutions they developed, and the culture they shared."[24] Lewis found that black residents in Norfolk (which is, interestingly, Josey's birthplace) were able to survive during the time of segregation because they successfully supported each other as a community.

Lewis theorized the notion of "congregation" in a Jim Crow environment. Congregation was important because it "symbolized an act of free will, whereas segregation represented the imposition of another's will."[25] It provided for more space than power, and African Americans used this space to gather their cultural bearings and develop their leadership abilities. This was also true for Josey when he worked at predominantly black institutions. He says, "My years at Delaware State were formative, the seven years at Savannah State were momentous, both professionally and personally; above all, I reached self-hood and manhood and, working with Black people in Georgia."[26] When Josey left the FLP in 1954, he also left librarianship for a year to enter the world of academia at Savannah State College.[27] This move reaffirmed his love of libraries and his desire to work in them. Thus, he returned to librarianship the following year and took on the challenge of promoting academic libraries at Delaware State College Library.[28]

DELAWARE STATE COLLEGE

Delaware State College (now University) is located in the capital city of Dover. It was established by the Delaware General Assembly on May 15, 1891, as "The Delaware College for Colored Students." It was created in response to the Morrill Act of 1890, which required that states either open their land-grant colleges to all races or establish a separate land-grant educational facility for African Americans. Full accreditation was granted in 1957 and has been maintained since.[29] The University of Delaware in Wilmington, the largest university in the state, did not begin enrolling blacks until 1948.[30] The college was elevated to university status and was renamed Delaware State University in 1993.[31] Recruited for the position of librarian and assistant professor at Delaware State College in September of 1955, Josey was hired to help get the school accredited.[32] They had lost their accreditation the year prior because the library was not up to standards. After he successfully obtained certification for the library two years later, he wrote about the process, officially launching his career as an author.

A series of articles that he published while at Delaware State College is worth noting because they provide a lens into Josey's early formation as a library leader. One of Josey's first publications, "College Library Accreditation: Boom or Bust," was published in 1957 in the widely read *Wilson Library Bulletin*.[33] Written for library managers, this article describes in detail the accreditation processes he encountered at the Delaware State Library. His analysis provided the reader with the tools necessary for library accreditation. Josey enjoyed the accreditation process. He believed it gave him the opportunity to reevaluate the role of the library in relation to the overall college. It also provided the opportunity for the administrators and other faculty to recognize the importance and viability of the library. He contends, "The necessity for a new look at the library's program and a re-evaluation of its role as an integral part of the total educational picture raises the library to the level of that lofty plane of 'the heart of the college.'"[34] His vision was not only to gain accreditation for the library; he wanted to promote the use of the library and highlight the library as an asset to the entire academic community.

The relevance and value of the academic library to the university has been a perennial concern for librarians since the rise of American research universities in the nineteenth century. While the priority of the library has changed from merely protecting books in the seventeenth century to providing instruction and services to their users in the nineteenth century, many librarians like Josey struggled with bringing users into the library to use its resources. Recently, accrediting bodies have attempted to streamline their university standards to eliminate any mention of libraries or the integration of the work librarians do. For example, in 2014, "The Middle States standards set the bar for the accreditation of colleges in five states, the District of Columbia, Puerto Rico, and the U.S. Virgin Islands."[35] If the resolution was adopted, the new standards would have shaped "higher education in four of the eight Ivy League universities, the top two largest U.S. colleges as measured by enrollment, nine Historically Black Colleges, and the first college in the U.S. dedicated to the education of the deaf."[36] The Association of College and Research Libraries (ACRL) took a stand on this issue and with the assistance of the many professional librarians and the ALA, they were successful in amending the accreditation guidelines to include language that embraces the value of library services.

During his tenure at Delaware State College, Josey became convinced that young students from marginalized communities should be exposed to great literary scholars. With the financial backing of the president of the college, he created the "Library Culture Series."[37] This innovative program provided honoraria and transportation for distinguished black writers to visit the Delaware State College campus. Authors such as Langston Hughes, Kay Boyle, Elizabeth Vroman, and many others gave presentations to the library community of students and faculty.[38] Josey wrote about his efforts in an article titled "A College Library's Cultural Series."[39] He described the programs he implemented to promote reading of noncurricular materials; here he stressed the importance of reading—not just academic reading but reading for leisure. The goal was that lectures from these literary greats would encourage students to do more reading not related to the curriculum. Josey believed that his small college library could be more than a depository for books. He argued that "it c[ould] transform itself into a battleground for ideas by offering forums, lectures, debates, book reviews, etc."[40] He advocated that the library could reach out to those in the community:

> Exhibition of books that relate to the topics discussed at an open forum makes the students, faculty, and members of the community aware of the resources of the library, thus enabling the library to advertise its wares. Since the college library had a stake in liberal education, it is fitting and proper that programs similar to the Library Cultural Series should be part and parcel of college library service.[41]

The idea of reaching out to the neighboring community may have come from Josey's earlier experience working as a public librarian. The "Library Culture Series" lectures were similar to programs typically found in public libraries. Another program he promoted at the library during his tenure as director was an exhibition he showcased for a recruitment day in 1958. A discussion about this innovative program was published in *Library Journal* in 1958.[42] The display was used as a way for the library to garner the attention of visiting parents. Josey felt that the library should do more than just open its doors; he believed the library staff should be innovative in attracting prospective students and parents to the college library. One exhibit was the "Useful Atom," a package exhibit "assembled by the American Museum of Atomic Energy with a library set-up in mind."[43] Josey also brought books to the exhibit because he wanted to show the importance of reading.[44] The success of the exhibit demonstrated Josey's innovativeness and his leadership early in his career as a librarian. His intention was to share the exhibit with high school teachers and their students; he believed that in so doing, it helped strengthen the relationship of the college with other teachers working at the high-school level. As Josey recalled, "Several science teachers visited the campus for the first time just to see the exhibit."[45] There was one "visit by a science teacher and his class from the northern part of the state, whose students ha[d] not had a history of coming to Delaware State College."[46]

Josey was active in the state library association, and Delaware State College was the setting for one of its annual conferences. It was the first time the association met at Delaware State College, and the first time most of the white members of the Delaware Library Association had ever visited the Delaware campus. Josey assumed the role of editor of the *Delaware Library Association Bulletin* when the former editor took a position in another state, giving him the honor of being the first African American to edit the state magazine.[47] Because of Josey's great success in getting the library accredited and his active role in librarianship in the state, the Delaware State Department of Public Instruction appointed him to a statewide school librarian certification revision committee.

Josey spoke of his time at Delaware State College as his "formative years," and the seven years following at Savannah State College as "momentous, both professionally and personally."[48] It was during his first year in Delaware that he married Dorothy Johnson, and in 1954, a year later, his only child, Elaine Jacqueline, was born. Following in her father's footsteps, Elaine Jacqueline Josey attended Howard University and has been active in civil rights issues most of her life. Also, following in the footsteps of her father, she is the former executive director of the North Carolina branch of the NAACP.[49] Although Josey and his wife divorced after seven years, they remained friends. He warmly acknowledged her during his 1984 ALA presidential inaugural address.[50]

Josey left Delaware State College after four years of service, mainly because he received a letter from the president of Savannah State College inviting him to return because they were building a new library and they wanted him to oversee it. Savannah State College had a building that was designated exclusively for library services.[51] Like most historic black institutions, the Savannah State College did not have much money. Josey was known for saying "they were interested in training the brawn rather than training the mind" because they preferred to build gymnasiums rather than libraries.[52]

It was at the Delaware State College Library that Josey began to emerge as a leader.

SAVANNAH STATE COLLEGE

Savannah State College was originally founded because of the Second Morrill Land Grant Act on August 30, 1890. The act mandated that Southern states develop black land-grant colleges.[53] In 1996, the Board of Regents of the University System of Georgia elevated Savannah State College to state university status, and the school's name was changed to Savannah State University.[54] In July 1959, Josey accepted the position of librarian and associate professor at Savannah State College.[55] One of the first tasks that Josey faced was to assess the professional staff members' duties and responsibilities. To this end, he made several significant changes to their job descriptions in order to help increase the workflow of the new library.[56]

Among the many procedures implemented, he created a position of circulation librarian and librarian counselor. Josey believed it was important to have a person available to assist students with basic library instruction because so many of the students came from schools in neighboring communities with poor libraries or did not have access to local public libraries due to the segregated practices in the state. Because Josey had similar experiences growing up in Portsmouth, Virginia, he was able to bring an understanding to this situation like few others. Josey also realized that he needed to increase the staff in order to perform the core functions of an academic library. Thus, he created several positions for the new library, including clerical assistants and student workers.[57]

Despite the committed library staff, Josey felt the library had taken a passive role on campus prior to his arrival.[58] His years at Delaware State College had aptly prepared him to take on the challenges at Savannah State College. He understood that if the library was going to support the instructional and research programs of the college, it had to have more visibility and

Figure 3.3. Library staff at Savannah State College Library. *Special Collections of Asa H. Gordon Library, Savannah State University*

more of a meaningful role in the lives of students, faculty, and the college community. Therefore, Josey set out to change the image of the library so that it would become a "vital organ of an institution of higher learning."[59] In order to accomplish this goal, Josey adopted a vigorous public relations agenda and implemented programs that he designed at the Delaware State College Library.

He also created new programs that were specifically targeted for Savannah State College. The purpose of the publicity campaign was to promote the services of the library to the students, faculty, and the overall academic community. In particular, two programs were the Great Books Discussion Group and the Library Lecture Series. These programs attracted large numbers of whites into the Savannah State College campus for the first time and garnered national recognition from the ALA. The Savannah State College Library was twice the recipient of the John Cotton Dana Library Public Relations Award.[60] During the ALA annual conference in 1962, these awardees were cited as outstanding among college and university libraries "for a publicity program geared to integrate the services of the library with the faculty, students, and college community."[61] Savannah State College was recognized again in 1964 at the ALA conference in St. Louis, Missouri, for a "varied, vigorous program of interesting scope in a college library with limited resources."[62]

One of Josey's goals as the new director was to make the institution into more of a center of intellectual life for the campus community. As such, he wanted to improve the reading skills of students prior to their arrival on campus. He believed that many of the incoming freshmen would be intimidated by the number of textbooks used in an academic setting and that students would not be inclined to do a lot of reading.

He devised a plan that would examine the reading habits of incoming freshmen. The study originated from a shared vision among the faculty that Savannah State College wanted to promote books and reading. Josey compiled a list of twenty-five books that he perceived to be of crucial importance. This list was sent to new students over several consecutive summers. Findings from the survey revealed that the reading list encouraged more independent reading and proved to be the stimulus for more independent study and use of library materials. As a result, the library reported an increase in circulation from 20 to 39 percent. These efforts speak to Josey's clear vision to assist individuals with independent thinking and learning. Making a core set of readings available to students ahead of time would help those who engaged in reading to gain confidence before they arrived on campus and courses began.

In his mission to make the library more significant, Josey made challenges to the faculty that were not always well received. He and staff conducted a study of the faculty's use of the library and found it extremely limited. He was convinced that underprivileged young black people who had not had the opportunity to use good libraries needed to see their professors use the library. He was a firm believer that "a professor educates as much by what he does as by what he teaches."[63] This conviction was reinforced by his experiences at the Delaware State College Library and Savannah State College and led him to publish an article titled "The Absent Professors" in *Library Journal.*[64] This outspoken article earned him much respect from many librarians (both black and white) because they shared his view; he received more than fifty letters from college and university librarians who said that his experiences were similar to their own.[65]

Findings of the study were reported at a faculty meeting and consequently made some faculty enemies for Josey.[66] The chair of the English department was upset with Josey's tactics and wrote him a scathing letter that said, "You will note that the attitude of the department is student-centered and not library-centered."[67] As one who rarely backs down to a challenge, Josey quoted this letter in his study in "The Role of the College Library Staff in the Instruction in the Use of the Library," published as an article in an issue of the *College and Research Libraries* in 1962.[68]

Josey also took on the role of mentor for librarians while at Savannah State College. In the spring of 1960, he and Madeline Harrison (the technical processing librarian at Savannah State College) organized a teacher-librarian curriculum. This program brought approximately forty in-service teachers from the southwest Georgia area to the college. Although it was designed to train elementary school librarians, it also provided librarians from high schools in Georgia and South Carolina with training. Josey obtained a grant from the Southern Education Foundation for thirty teachers to study this course during the summers of 1962 and 1963. The program received accreditation from the Georgia State Department of Education for five years and was modestly successful, considering that it sponsored what was one of the first programs of its kind in the city of Savannah. Josey also encouraged Georgians to pursue librarianship as a career and was able to persuade his longtime secretary to become a librarian. "I was able to encourage many able students to go on to graduate library schools, and I can point with pride to about twenty librarians who now have their graduate library degrees who began their study in the [Savannah State College] program."[69]

Josey's time at the Free Library of Philadelphia, Delaware State College, and Savannah State College provided him with a foundation for his future career in library and information science, but it is also provided a platform for the emergence of a leader.

The civil rights movement was the perfect backdrop for Josey's rise to leadership. When he arrived at the Savannah State College Library to begin his tenure as director in 1959,[70] Georgia, like other states in the Deep South, was undergoing racial turmoil. As one of the strongest slaveholding states prior to the Civil War, Georgia was among the states to secede from the Union in 1861. After the Civil War, racial tension and national conflict became almost inseparable in the state, and the state government found other ways to keep black and white citizens separated, even without slavery. Throughout Georgia, and across the South, Jim Crow laws institutionalized segregation and came to define expectations in Georgia, as blacks were routinely denied the right to share public spaces and other opportunities.[71]

Blacks fought segregation as soon as it began. Although the modern civil rights movement is often marked as beginning with the 1954 Supreme Court decision banning school segregation, or the day in 1955 when Rosa Parks refused to move from a bus seat in Montgomery, Alabama, for many African Americans, it is thought to have begun with the start of WWII for the United States in 1941. Just like Josey, several black Americans signed up to fight in WWII and served with such distinction that President Harry S. Truman formally desegregated the military after the war. Black veterans returned to their homes in places like Georgia, filled with American pride and achievement, only to find strict racial segregation still in place. Averse to accept racial conditions any longer, black Georgians registered to vote in multitudes, defying the traditional threats and prohibitions that had prevented them in the past. By the end of 1946, Georgia had registered more than 14,000 new black voters.[72]

As the civil rights movement progressed, black leaders in Georgia organized around churches and other grassroots institutions. Protests, rallies, and other events to combat segregation were widespread. However, white supremacy intensified in the 1950s as supporters of segregation rallied. Governor Herman Talmadge strengthened Jim Crow laws, restricted the rights of blacks to vote, and attempted to outlaw pro–civil rights groups. Nevertheless, civil rights persisted with victories in 1954 when all public schools across the country were formally desegregated. The city of Savannah achieved recognition for this in the early 1960s when a massive campaign led by local NAACP leader W. W. Law forced widespread desegregation. Savannah soon became a national leader in voluntary desegregation, gaining recognition from King as the most desegregated city in the South.

With racial tensions at its highest peak, it was no surprise when organizations like the NAACP came to the aid of Savannahians. Founded in 1909, the NAACP was formed partly in response to the continuing horrendous practice of lynching and the 1908 race riot in Springfield, Illinois. In that event, two black men being held in a Springfield jail for alleged crimes against white people were surreptitiously transferred to a jail in another city, spurring a white mob to burn down forty homes in Springfield's black residential district, ransack local businesses, and murder two African Americans. Disgusted at the violence that was committed against blacks, a group of white liberals that included Mary White Ovington and Oswald Garrison Villard (both the descendants of abolitionists) William English Walling, and Henry Moscowitz, issued a call for a meeting in New York City to discuss racial justice. Sixty people responded to the call, seven of whom were African American (including Du Bois, Ida B. Wells-Barnett, and Mary Church Terrell.[73]

Just like the aforementioned trailblazers, Josey emerged as a leader not only among librarians but also within the broader civil rights movement. Bernard M. Bass asserts that "[a] transformational leader with idealized attributes displays a sense of power and confidence and is able to reassure others that they can overcome obstacles."[74] He further contends "The members or team of the organization often emulates leaders who possess idealized influence, viewing the leader as a charismatic personification of the values and mission of that organization."[75]

Josey not only saw his role as a leader on the issues facing librarians, but also as an antagonist to the injustice he experienced and witnessed. He says, "In my attempt to disturb the intellectual sterility and apathy at Savannah State [College], I made many faculty friends and some faculty enemies."[76] This quote by Josey in many ways exemplified his philosophy and is aligned with the sentiments of his colleagues throughout his career. He challenged those who took a passive stance on issues he believed to be critical. He was a man who continually stood for his convictions and who did not hesitate to disrupt the status quo. While there were many who adored him and his feisty approach to bringing about change, there were others who did not approve of his method. Nevertheless, many would concede that he was always acting on what he believed was best for the library profession.

SAVANNAH STATE COLLEGE ACTIVISM

Josey rocked the intellectual sterility at Savannah State College through his activism in the civil rights movement in the city of Savannah. As a board member of the NAACP, he participated in several measures to end discrimination. Most notable was his opposition to the Anti-Picketing Ordinance. Fifteen months prior to enactment of the law, the black citizens of Savannah struggled with boycotts, cross burnings, and oppositional measures to overturn segregated practices of Jim Crow. The law has its genesis in the actions of four African American freshmen from North Carolina A&T College, who went into a Woolworth's store and staged a sit-in. When told they would not be served, they refused to leave, and this sparked a movement in the South. Black students in colleges throughout the South saw the incident on television and began sit-ins in their own towns. Students demanded desegregated lunch counters and equal employment opportunities; they also wanted blacks to be addressed in a courteous businesslike manner and the release of thirty-three arrested protestors.[77]

The local merchants refused the students' demands, and the local NAACP branch initiated a boycott of local businesses.[78] The state legislature enacted a "'[t]respass [l]aw' which made it a misdemeanor for any person or group to refuse to leave the premises of an establishment when asked to do so by the proprietor."[79] Furthermore, the city council passed an anti-picketing ordinance and the mayor affirmed that the law would stay in effect regardless of whether it violated constitutional rights.[80]

Taking issue with this, Josey wrote an editorial in the local Savannah black paper opposing the law and challenging its merit. He highlighted that businesses had closed and the Supreme Court outlawed a state law prohibiting picketing in Alabama; the Supreme Court ruled that picketing was equated to free speech and upheld that it was an activity protected by the First Amendment.[81] His editorial in the *Savannah Tribune* "gave hope and confidence to [the] pickets, [Josey] believe[d], at the same time put the Savannah business and political leadership on notice that the black community meant business and would fight the Anti-Picketing Ordinance all the way to the Supreme Court."[82] However, shortly thereafter, the ordinance was dissolved because several stores were forced to close due to the city's evaporating economy.

Josey was often approached to advise student groups on campus. He was the faculty advisor for the debate team and for Alpha Phi Omega fraternity, and he was instrumental in helping students establish a chapter of the NAACP.[83] The African American community of Savannah united behind the young students, and the local branch of the NAACP supported them by providing bail and launching a series of meetings that set the foundation for the student chapter. However, the faculty did not all support the sit-ins. Some faculty believed that the protests destroyed the progress that had been made thus far.[84] Nonetheless, Josey supported the students regardless of the fallout from his colleagues.[85] In 2001, he recalled:

> One of my momentous occasions involving the civil rights movement in Savannah was one that I'll never forget. The leaders of the NAACP decided to bring in Martin Luther King to speak. . . . King at the time was pastoring in Montgomery, Alabama, and Reverend Curtis Jackson who was a minister in Savannah at the time had about sixteen of us at his house for dinner before the mass meeting. I had the pleasant surprise to have been seated next to King. It was an experience I'll never forget. He was the most humane person I've ever met. His spirituality and his love for people and what he was doing just exuded from his body. You could feel that you're in a presence of a Gandhi or something like that. That was the kind of impact he had on me. King knew who I was surprisingly enough because we had a woman named Mercedes Wright who had been going around nationally helping to start boycotts. And, so in one

of her speeches she talked about what the students at Savannah State and their courageous librarian had done. I didn't even know. He was sacrificing himself because the state could fire him at any moment because he was violating segregation laws. So, King had heard about me and so going around the table introducing us, I said, "I'm E. J. Josey." He said, "Well, you're the librarian, I know who you are." From then on, I just burst all my buttons off my shirt, being so proud. [86]

In 2016, the Georgia Historical Society commemorated the Savannah Protest Movement that highlights the efforts by students and the community leaders during the 1960s:

On March 16, 1960, black students led by the NAACP Youth Council staged sit-ins at white-only lunch counters in eight downtown stores. Three students, Carolyn Quilloin, Ernest Robinson, and Joan Tyson, were arrested in the Azalea Room here at Levy's Department Store (now SCAD's Jen Library). In response, African American leaders W. W. Law, Hosea Williams, and Eugene Gadsden organized a nearly complete boycott of city businesses and led voter registration drives that helped elect a moderate city. [87]

Figure 3.4.   Josey with the student chapter of the NAACP at Savannah State College. *Special Collections of Asa H. Gordon Library, Savannah State University*

LEADING THE BUREAU OF THE STATE OF NEW YORK

Drawing from eleven years of experience as the director of two academic libraries, Josey was cognizant of the need for libraries to pool their resources, and he firmly believed that no one academic library could solely satisfy the library research needs of its users.[88] Therefore, it was no surprise when he left Savannah State College for the Division of Library Development at the New York State Library in Albany, New York. Josey was invited to the New York State Department of Education because of his leadership in community outreach.[89] At Savannah State College, he was known for hosting writers like James Baldwin in order to bring in people from the outside of the college to the library.[90] As chair of the ACRL in 1966, Josey presented a committee report at the ACRL meeting at Queens College in New York, and afterward was approached by Basil Miller, a librarian whom he had met working at the Journalism Library at Columbia University, and Jean Connor, who was the director in charge of the vision of library development at the New York State Library. Both librarians were in the process of establishing the Bureau of College and Research Libraries as a new system that mirrored their already successful public library one. Although Josey was initially reluctant to leave Savannah, he was eventually persuaded to go to Albany.

State library agencies are the official bureaus of a state or territory; they are charged with the extension and development of public library services throughout the area and have authority under law to administer plans in accordance with the provisions of the Library Services and Technology Act.[91] During the 1960s, the state of New York had one of the most progressive state library systems in the nation. It set the standard for other agencies in the country and was on the cutting edge of library development.[92] The Division of Library Development provides statewide leadership and advisory services to all libraries—public, school, academic, and special—throughout the state of New York. It is a major unit of the New York State Library and is located in the Office of Cultural Education within the New York State Education Department. The New York State Library has two divisions: library development and the research library. Both serve the people and the libraries of the state.

Josey began his career with the Division of Library Development as an associate in the Bureau of Academic and Research Libraries in September 1966. Two years later, he received a provisional appointment as Chief of the Bureau of Academic and Research Libraries, and two additional years later the appointment was made permanent.[93] During this time, there were very few African American professionals working in state library agencies. As a pioneer in this arena of librarianship, Josey wanted to exceed expectations so that he would succeed in a position of leadership that was traditionally held by white professionals.[94] State library agencies provided a variety of advisory roles that supported the library services in the state. New York had one of the most progressive state library agencies, with its cooperative library network development during the 1960s.[95]

During his first three months in his new position, Josey focused on developing and improving the services for the 216 academic and research libraries in New York.[96] The Board of Regents for New York during this time approved a proposal for long-range planning for all of the academic libraries including those of the universities, such as Columbia, Cornell, and New York University, to strengthen academic library service in the state up to year 2000.[97] The Reference and Research Library Resources Program (or, as it was commonly known, the 3Rs system: reference, research, resources) was a cooperative reference and research regional library network that aimed to meet the needs of research and the university scholar.[98] The primary goal was to bring all the academic and research libraries in the state of New York into a cooperative system so that scholars, "regardless of geographic location, would have access to all of the library resources in the state."[99] The development of the statewide component of the 3Rs program and contractual service arrangement, such as the New York State Interlibrary Loan Program, which was the main component of the 3Rs program, was one of two state-compensated interlibrary loan programs in the nation.

Kathleen Weibel, a librarian and a longtime women's rights activist, first met Josey at a meeting for the Social Responsibility Round Table (SRRT) in the late 1960s. In 1968, Weibel was hired to develop the continuing education program at the Division of Library Development. She was supervised by Josey, and she remembers how effective he was as a manager at work:

> He adapted his supervision style to fit me which I think you have to do as a supervisor. His leadership style in ALA was different than his leadership style in the state library. His leadership style in the state of New York was in between those two things. What I found real intriguing about him was this sort of free spirit. It was very bureaucratic, very hierarchical, that's my view and he could manage to get things done. . . . I think he's able to read situations, which is what a leader needs to be able to do. He can read the situation and figure out how to get things done. He can build coalitions and alliances. People hold him in very high respect because of his personal dignity.[100]

Because of Josey's personal experiences, he emerged as a strong advocate for librarianship. Early on in his professional career, he held leadership roles that helped propel him to become an effective spokesperson for the profession. His deep commitment to the philosophy, aims, and objectives of librarianship are mirrored by his own personal values of living in a democratic society.

Since his early years in Delaware and Georgia, Josey gave charitably of his time and talents in serving on a variety of ALA and New York Library

Association committees. A sampling of the list discloses extensive involvement: ALA Nominating Committee, ALA Ad Hoc Committee on Equal Opportunity, Editorial Board of the *ALA Yearbook*, and ACRL Intellectual Freedom Committee.[101] After seven years at Savannah State College, Josey wanted an opportunity to serve the profession in an integrated capacity and an opportunity presented itself to become involved in cooperative library development. He believed that "the development of library networks and of consultative services to college, university, and special libraries must be the responsibility of a State Agency."[102]

In Albany, Josey continued his work with the NAACP. In 1980, he was elected vice president of the Albany Branch and again the following year due to his leadership and successful organization of protesting the South African Springbok rugby team playing at the Albany Sports Arena. Josey believed that permitting a team that supported South African apartheid was an affront to the sensitivity of citizens in New York. Apartheid was a systemic effort of institutional racism in South Africa from 1948 to 1994.[103] He rallied the media and organized a mass protest that resulted in the governor issuing an executive order forbidding the team from playing in Albany.[104] Josey was elected president of the Albany branch of the NAACP the following year and was successful during his tenure staging sit-ins and protesting against US policies in South Africa.[105] Friend and colleague Jim F. McCoy recalls, "the KKK [was] recruiting" in Brattleboro, Vermont, and "[t]hrough [Josey] the Albany Branch sent a large contingent as part of the counter-demonstration."[106] He further asserts, "For [Josey] it was imperative that the NAACP maintain a presence whenever injustice and discrimination reared its ugly head. . . . His eye was always on the 'prize,' elimination of racism within the library profession and his community."[107]

The years that Josey spent at Delaware State College, Savannah State College, and the New York Department Board of Education were not only formative for him in his professional career but also transformative for those who worked with him. It can be argued that the four tenets of Bass' transformational leadership theory can be viewed within the context of Josey's early career. However, intellectual stimulation specifically characterizes this period in his life. It was at these educational institutions where he not only challenged the prevailing conventions of how work was done in the academic libraries where he worked by revitalizing programming and bringing in literary greats to increase library usage, but he also encouraged his employees and librarians around the nation to do the same.

Josey essentially became a teacher among librarians by creating a blueprint for others to follow. Bringing literary artists and celebrities into libraries is common practice today. One example can be seen shortly after Carla Hayden, Josey's protégé, became Librarian of Congress. She, along with staff member Nicholas Brown, hosted a tribute series, "Library of Congress

Figure 3.5. E. J. Josey speaking in front of the Capitol Building, circa 1960.
Courtesy of the University of Illinois Archives: ALA0002095

Bibliodiscotheque" that featured a concert by recording artist Gloria Gaynor and the "music, dance and fashion represented in the national collections."[108] Similarly, his leadership at the New York Department of Education can also be viewed as transformational: Josey spearheaded and implemented the New York State ILL system, which was essentially the state version of WorldCat, a global collective catalog that allows access to collections of more than 72,000 libraries around the world.[109] His efforts were innovative and forward thinking, especially when considering the time, which was the latter part of the 1960s and prior to the digital age.

NOTES

1. Brown v. Board of Education, 347 U.S. 483 (1954), 494.

2. Civil Rights Act of 1964, Pub. L. No. 88–352, 78 Stat. 241; *see* Wayne A. Wiegand and Shirley A. Wiegand, *The Desegregation of Public Libraries in the Jim Crow South: Civil Rights and Local Activism* (Baton Rouge: Louisiana State University Press, 2018), 6–13.

3. Wiegand and Wiegand, *Desegregation of Public Libraries in the Jim Crow South*, 13.

4. Plessy v. Ferguson, 163 U.S. 537 (1896), *overruled by* Brown v. Board of Education, 347 U.S. 483 (1954).

5. E. J. Josey and Marva L. DeLoach, eds., *Handbook of Black Librarianship*, 2nd ed. (Lanham, MD: Scarecrow Press, 2000), ix; Casper LeRoy Jordan and E. J. Josey, "A Chronology of Events in Black Librarianship," in *Handbook of Black Librarianship*, ed. E. J. Josey and Marva L. DeLoach, 2nd ed. (Lanham, MD: Scarecrow Press, 2000), 3–4.

6. Greg Landgraf, "Blazing Trails: Pioneering African-American Librarians Share Their Stories," *American Libraries*, January 2, 2018, https://americanlibrariesmagazine.org/2018/01/02/blazing-trails/.

7. Free Library of Philadelphia, "History of the Library," accessed June 18, 2018, http://www.library.phila.gov/about/history.htm.

8. Free Library of Philadelphia, "History of the Library."

9. Susan Stamberg, "How Andrew Carnegie Turned His Fortune into a Library Legacy," August 1, 2013, https://www.npr.org/2013/08/01/207272849/how-andrew-carnegie-turned-his-fortune-into-a-library-legacy.

10. Free Library of Philadelphia, "History of the Library."

11. Free Library of Philadelphia, "History of the Library."

12. Free Library of Philadelphia, "History of the Library."

13. Matthew J. Countryman, *Up South: Civil Rights and Black Power in Philadelphia* (Philadelphia: University of Pennsylvania Press, 2006), 13.

14. E. J. Josey, "A Dreamer—with a Tiny Spark," in *The Black Librarian in America*, ed. E. J. Josey (Metuchen, NJ: Scarecrow Press, 1970), 300–301.

15. Clara Stanton Jones, "E. J. Josey: Librarian for All Seasons," in *E. J. Josey: An Activist Librarian*, ed. Ismail Abdullahi (Metuchen, NJ: Scarecrow Press, 1992), 3.

16. E. J. Josey, personal interview with the author, April 6, 2007.

17. Josey, "Dreamer," 301.

18. Josey, "Dreamer," 302.

19. Josey, "Dreamer," 301–2.

20. Josey, "Dreamer," 301–2.

21. Josey, "Dreamer," 302.

22. Jones, "E. J. Josey," 3.

23. Josey, "Dreamer," 302–3.

24. Earl Lewis, *In Their Own Interests: Race, Class, and Power in Twentieth-Century Norfolk, Virginia* (Berkeley: University of California Press, 1991), 3.

25. Lewis, *In Their Own Interests*, 92.

26. Josey, "Dreamer," 304.

27. Josey, "Dreamer," 302.

28. Josey, "Dreamer," 302–3.

29. "Delaware State University: History," accessed November 27, 2007, http://www.desu.edu/about/history.

30. James Newton, "Black Americans in Delaware: An Overview," accessed July 30, 2018, http://www1.udel.edu/BlackHistory/overview.html.

31. "Delaware State University."

32. Josey, "Dreamer," 302–3.

33. E. J. Josey, "College Library Accreditation: Boom or Bust," *Wilson Library Bulletin* 32, no. 3 (November 1957): 233–34.

34. Josey, "College Library Accreditation," 233.

35. Beth Evans, "Accreditation Standards & Libraries: A Dangerous Ride down a Devolving Course," ACRLog, January 27, 2014, https://acrlog.org/2014/01/27/accreditation-standards-libraries-a-dangerous-ride-down-a-devolving-course/.

36. Evans, "Accreditation Standards & Libraries."

37. Josey, "Dreamer," 303.

38. Josey, "Dreamer," 303.

39. E. J. Josey, "A College Library's Cultural Series," *Wilson Library Bulletin* 30, no. 10 (June 1956): 767–68.

40. Josey, "College Library's Cultural Series," 768.

41. Josey, "College Library's Cultural Series," 768.

42. E. Junius Josey, "The College Library and the Atom," *Library Journal* 83, no. 9 (May 1958): 1341–43. Citation for entire article in *Library Journal*.

43. Josey, "College Library and the Atom," 1341.

44. Josey, "College Library and the Atom," 1342.

45. Josey, "College Library and the Atom," 1343.

46. Josey, "College Library and the Atom," 1343.

47. Josey, "Dreamer," 303.

48. E. J. Josey, personal interview with the author, April 8, 2007.

49. Elaine Jacqueline Josey-Turner, personal interview with the author, April 8, 2007.

50. E. J. Josey, "Forging Coalitions for the Public Good" (inaugural address, American Library Association, Dallas, TX, 1984).

51. Josey, "Dreamer," 302–3.

52. E. J. Josey, in personal communication with the author, March 14, 2001.

53. *Savannah State University 2005–2007 Catalog* (Savannah, GA: Savannah State University, 2005), 18, https://www.savannahstate.edu/academic-affairs/documents/catalog05-07undergraduate.pdf.

54. *Savannah State University 2005–2007 Catalog*, 19.

55. Josey, "Dreamer," 303.

56. Josey, "Dreamer," 304.

57. Josey, "Dreamer," 304.

58. Josey, "Dreamer," 304.

59. Josey, "Dreamer," 305; Josey, personal interview with the author, April 8, 2007.

60. Josey, "Dreamer," 305–6.

61. Josey, "Dreamer," 305.

62. Josey, "Dreamer," 305.

63. Josey, "Dreamer," 306.

64. E. J. Josey, "The Absent Professors," *Library Journal* 87, no. 2 (January 1962): 173–75, 181.

65. Josey, "Dreamer," 306.

66. Josey, "Dreamer," 306.

67. Josey, "Dreamer," 306.

68. E. J. Josey, "The Role of the College Library Staff in Instruction in the Use of the Library," *College and Research Libraries* 23, no. 6 (November 1962): 492–98, https://doi.org/10.5860/crl_23_06_492.

69. Josey, "Dreamer," 312.

70. Josey, "Dreamer," 303.

71. Albert B. Saye, *Georgia: History and Government*, rev. Teacher's ed. (Austin, TX: Steck-Vaughn Company, 1982), 135, 165–66, 219.

72. Robert A. Holmes, "Black Suffrage in the Twentieth Century," *New Georgia Encyclopedia*, last edited June 6, 2017, https://www.georgiaencyclopedia.org/articles/government-politics/black-suffrage-twentieth-century.

73. Library of Congress, "NAACP: A Century in the Fight for Freedom: Founding and Early Years," accessed June 20, 2019, https://www.loc.gov/exhibits/naacp/founding-and-early-years.html.

74. Tawney A. Hughes, "Idealized, Inspirational, and Intellectual Leaders in the Social Sector: Transformational Leadership and the Kravis Prize" (senior thesis, Claremont University, 2014), 8, http://scholarship.claremont.edu/cmc/_theses/906; *see* Bernard M. Bass, *Leadership and Performance beyond Expectations* (New York: Free Press, 1985), 14–32.

75. Hughes, "Idealized, Inspirational, and Intellectual Leaders in the Social Sector," 8; *see* Bass, *Leadership and Performance beyond Expectations*, 14–32.

76. Josey, "Dreamer," 306.

77. Josey, "Dreamer," 308–11.

78. Josey, "Dreamer," 308.

79. Josey, "Dreamer," 308.

80. Josey, "Dreamer," 308.

81. Josey, "Dreamer," 310–11.

82. Josey, "Dreamer," 311.

83. Josey, "Dreamer," 308.

84. Josey, "Dreamer," 309.

85. James Eaton, personal interview with the author, December 6, 2007.

86. E. J. Josey, in personal communication with the author, March 10, 2001.

87. The Georgia Civil Rights Trail: Savannah Protest Movement Historical Marker Dedication, https://georgiahistory.com/education-outreach/historical-markers/hidden-histories/the-georgia-civil-rights-trail-the-savannah-protest-movement/.

88. Josey, "Dreamer," 319.

89. Josey, "Dreamer," 319–20.

90. Josey, "Dreamer," 307.

91. Library Services and Technology Act, Pub. L. 94–462, tit. II, subtit. B, as added Pub. L. No. 104–208, div. A, tit. I, sec. 101(e) [tit. VII, sec. 702], 110 Stat. 3009–233, 3009–295 (1996).

92. Josey, in personal communication with the author, March 10, 2001.

93. Josey, "Dreamer," 319.

94. Josey, in personal communication with the author, March 10, 2001.

95. Robert B. Ford, "A Pioneer in a State Library Agency: The New York Years, 1966–1986," in *E. J. Josey: An Activist Librarian,* ed. Ismail Abdullahi (Metuchen, NJ: Scarecrow Press, 1992), 40.

96. Ford, "A Pioneer in a State Library Agency," 40.

97. Ford, "A Pioneer in a State Library Agency," 40.

98. Ford, "A Pioneer in a State Library Agency," 40; Josey, "Dreamer," 318.

99. Ford, "A Pioneer in a State Library Agency," 41.

100. Kathleen Weibel, personal interview with the author, April 10, 2007.

101. Jones, "E. J. Josey: Librarian for All Seasons," 1–20.

102. Josey, "Dreamer," 319.

103. Al Kagan, "ALA, IFLA, and South Africa," *Progressive Librarian: A Journal for Critical Studies and Progressive Politics in Librarianship* 46 (Winter 2017/2018): 63–65, http://www.progressivelibrariansguild.org/PL/PL46/063kagan.pdf.

104. Jim F. McCoy, "Remembrances and Reflections of an NAACP Leader," in *E. J. Josey: An Activist Librarian*, ed. Ismail Abdullahi (Metuchen, NJ: Scarecrow Press, 1992), 123.

105. McCoy, "Remembrances and Reflections of an NAACP Leader," 123–24.

106. McCoy, "Remembrances and Reflections of an NAACP Leader," 124.

107. McCoy, "Remembrances and Reflections of an NAACP Leader," 124.

108. Andrew Chow, Gloria Gaynor to Perform at Library of Congress, *New York Times*, March 26, 2017.

109. WorldCat, OCLC, http://www.oclc.org.

Chapter Four

A Leader Rises Up

It is often said that in turbulent times, leaders rise to the challenge. Josey was no exception. During the pinnacle of his leadership in the ALA, he fought two systems of institutionalized racism: segregation in the United States and apartheid in South Africa. These systemic challenges dictated the need for someone to step forward to fight for justice.

To fully appreciate the significance of these occasions, it is important to understand the racial tensions that persisted in the ALA as an organization. Consequently, a history of ALA and the actions led by Josey is crucial to understanding his transformative leadership.

CIVIL RIGHTS IN LIBRARIANSHIP

The ALA was founded in 1876 with the goal of "provid[ing] leadership for the development, promotion and improvement of library and information services and the profession of librarianship in order to enhance learning and ensure access to information for all."[1] The professional ethics and values of the ALA were formulated early in the institution's history. Leaders and librarians of the organization were members of the "cultivated" classes who set the tone and spirit of the association.[2] The tradition of American professional organizations is closely tied to the perception that these institutions should be open to all without regard to social background. However, this was not the case where these organizations barred membership to many African American librarians and provided tacit support for mainstream culture of white dominance.

Mainstream institutions, such as the ALA, do not reflect the diverse cultures and values of the larger society. Rather, they mirror the ideals of the dominant culture. As Claud Anderson asserts, "Institutions were the means of inculcating values that would perpetually maintain the self-interest of European whites and their descendants."[3] Prior to the birth of the civil rights movement, the ALA was never confronted with the issue of racial discrimination. Similar to many other American institutions, it required advocacy from those who shared in the vision of racial equality to make change.

The ALA is an organization established on the core principles of democracy and free access to information. The ALA's Library Bill of Rights, adopted in 1939, advocated that "[a] person's right to use a library should not be denied or abridged because of origin, age, background, or views."[4] Unfortunately, these values were not always practiced by librarians or members of the association. Nonetheless, ALA as an organization welcomed black members and was never segregated.

Segregation did not become a "real" issue for the ALA until 1936 when the annual conference was held for the first time in the South. The first published account of discrimination in the ALA occurred at the 1936 ALA Annual Meeting in Richmond, Virginia. In an effort to obtain a large turnout, black librarians received invitations from the Richmond Local Arrangements Committee to attend the conference. It was not conveyed, however, that the participants would endure the segregated conditions of the city. Although African Americans were permitted to use the same hotel entrances as white conferees, they were not allowed access to conference halls or meetings that were held in dining areas in conjunction with meals. Additionally, black members of the association were given reserved seating in a designated area of the meeting hall, thereby diminishing their capacity to fully take part in the conference. Due to many protests by delegates and state associations, the executive board appointed a committee to formulate policy to ensure that this form of discrimination would not occur again. As a result, signs were posted at future meetings that "in all rooms and halls assigned to the Association for use in connection with its conference, or otherwise under its control, all members shall be admitted upon terms of full equity."[5]

African American librarians also faced discrimination that denied them membership in Southern library associations. Virginia Lacy Jones, former dean of the School of Library Service, Atlanta University, wrote about her experiences when she applied for membership to the Georgia Library Association:

> Once, when I submitted a letter to apply for admission and sent the membership fee, the check was returned with a letter stating that the Association at that time did not have provision for me to become a member.[6]

Josey had a similar experience. After entering library school in 1952, he joined the ALA.[7] However, when he tried to join the Georgia Library Association, he too received a letter rejecting his application. It was not until

1965, after his protest against the Southern state library associations, that he was allowed membership, becoming the first African American librarian of the Georgia Library Association.[8] It is likely that this rejection fueled his frustration with his profession and provided great impetus for him taking on the association in the decades ahead.

The 1960s ushered in a new era in American history, giving birth to a new age for American librarianship as well. No longer did blacks settle for second-class citizenry. They, along with socially minded white Americans, placed pressure on the legal and political system to bring an end to state-supported segregation in all public places—including libraries. African American librarians would participate in sit-ins in libraries throughout the South. These events not only influenced the national mood but also motivated library professionals to fight for equality with the goal of ending segregation in their profession. National civil rights leader King particularly inspired Josey. He believed that if King could fight for civil rights within the broader social movement, then he certainly could lead the challenge against segregation in his profession.[9] As a librarian at the Savannah State College Library, he championed the cause to eradicate segregation on campus as well at the Savannah Public Library. He, along with other members of the NAACP, demanded that the mayor of Georgia appoint blacks to the Savannah Public Library Board. He was one of the first African Americans appointed to a position on the board.[10]

Some white library leaders, like Eric Moon (editor of the *Library Journal* at that time), contributed significantly to the inception of civil rights in librarianship. In 1960, Moon published an article, "Segregated Libraries," by Rice Estes, then librarian of the Pratt Institute, who challenged segregation in the South and questioned whether the ALA was doing all it could for black librarians. Moon followed with an editorial titled "The Silent Subject" that suggested that Library Services Act funds be withheld from those libraries whose services were not equally available to everyone.[11] Although the ALA did not respond immediately to Moon's editorial, that same year the association approved a survey that documented the lack of access by citizens to library services and emphasized restrictions based on race in the South.[12]

JOSEY'S HISTORIC RESOLUTION

Josey's statement at the 1962 Annual Conference urging the ALA to be more responsive to all of its members became the backdrop for major integration efforts at the 1964 Annual Conference.[13] The ALA Annual Conference held in St. Louis, Missouri, in July 1964, coincided with the passage of the Civil Rights Act of 1964[14] outlawing segregation. However, still vivid in the mind of Josey was the assassination of President John F. Kennedy several months prior and the incessant civil rights struggle for blacks. Nevertheless, Josey accepted the invitation to attend the conference to appear on the ACRL College Library Section's program, one on which few blacks were invited to participate.[15] At the conference, Josey attended the National Library Week Program. During the program, the ALA passed a motion honoring the Mississippi Library Association for their National Library Week activities, in spite of their failure to comply with the ALA policies on equal membership to all librarians. Josey was disturbed by this and, as he describes it, "I exploded."[16] He recalls, "I was upset because I remembered that three civil rights workers, Andrew Goodman, James Chaney, and Michael Schwerner, were murdered and their undiscovered bodies were somewhere in Mississippi and that the Mississippi Library Association had withdrawn from the ALA rather than permit membership to Blacks."[17] Josey openly opposed the award by saying this:

> I vigorously protest the award of Honorable Mention being bestowed upon Mississippi Library Association for its National Library Week efforts, for two reasons. Firstly, Mississippi has withdrawn from ALA affiliation. Secondly, no state association should enjoy the benefits of membership, and at the same time, repudiate the ideals and bylaws of the American Library Association. Therefore, I request that the award be withdrawn.[18]

Although his resolution was initially rejected, Josey introduced a more comprehensive resolution on the final day of the conference that stated:

> All ALA officers and ALA staff members should refrain from attending in their official capacity or at the expense of ALA the meetings of state associations which are unable to meet fully the requirements of chapter status in ALA.[19]

Moon seconded the motion,[20] and, as Josey describes it, "all hell broke loose."[21]

Several months after the motion passed, Josey was accepted as a member of the Georgia State Library Association. The remaining states of Alabama, Louisiana, and Mississippi opened their membership to black librarians, and this was an important victory toward acceptance.[22]

Subsequently, Josey demanded immediate action to eliminate discrimination against African American librarians and other librarians of color in Southern public libraries. Prior to challenges to the ALA on the issue of segregation, minority librarians were constrained by those who were in a position of power in the ALA. Black librarians soon realized that in order for change to occur, they needed to take control of their own destinies and vie for leadership roles in the association.

CONFRONTING BIAS IN THE ALA

Interestingly, Josey could have avoided "racial concerns in order to protect his personal acceptability for advancement to the ALA's highest offices."[23] However, he never avoided controversy. His understanding of historical events urged him toward advocacy for equality for people of color and other marginalized groups. Unquestionably, this was additional work added to the normal load of duties, but Josey accepted it without hesitation due to his deeply rooted beliefs in what was best for the association and the general society. In addition to the resolution that ultimately ended segregation of the Southern chapters in the ALA, Josey was involved in several other controversial issues in the association. A concern that literally divided the ALA for a number of years was the film *The Speaker*. This film was produced in 1977 by the Intellectual Freedom Committee.[24] Although *The Speaker* initially was intended to "explain the special role of the library in preserving and disseminating controversial works,"[25] the final product was a movie "based on the widely reported confrontation at Harvard University where there was vigorous opposition to presenting William Shockley as a speaker because of his expressed position on White supremacy/Black inferiority."[26] In *The Speaker,* this situation was transferred to a high school setting and focused on a speaker who believed in the mental inferiority of African Americans.[27]

While the ALA was concerned that the setting had changed since the initial discussion of the film, confronting the issue of racism and free speech resulted in an enormous controversy. To the astonishment of the ALA board members, who had approved the making of the film in preproduction, many librarians were upset with the final result. It soon became a bitter debate, and, despite the good intentions of the executive board, African American librarians became infuriated and boycotted the release of the film. Meanwhile, others objected, countering that banning the movie would be a form of censorship.[28]

Although Josey was not a member of the ALA Council, he often consulted with Clara Stanton Jones who held the office of president of ALA at the time. According to Sanford Berman, retired head cataloger and principal librarian at the Hennepin County Library in Minnesota, "Both Josey and Clara Stanton Jones were very vocal about their objections to the film *The Speaker*. Josey led members of the BCALA to oppose it. . . . Although there were a lot of other people that joined in the chorus, I would say he was the principal leader in combating that and with great articulation and fervor appropriately."[29] It is important to note that although it was understandable that African American librarians would protest *The Speaker*, the film was not an issue solely about race; it was also a challenge over First Amendment rights. The marriage of these two issues had tremendous implications for democracy and was the driving force behind Josey's challenges.

Similarly, Josey took issue with negative terminology in library cataloging subject headings (LCSH). The challenge was led by notable library activist Sanford Berman who, in 1971, created a list that included approximately 225 sexist and racist headings that required correction in order to stop perpetuating bias.[30] Berman and Josey began a collaboration that lasted for more than twenty years. Their goal was to replace terms like "Negro" and "Afro American" in the LCSH. When asked about their collaboration, Berman remarked,

> [Josey] was able to supply authoritative contacts and correspondence and then his own statements which are powerful. These affected people and community speaking and so that led all the more credibility and weight to my arguments as they should have. So, it was truly that sort of a joint collaboration.[31]

After several years of working on numerous committees in the ALA, as well as serving on the council and the executive board, Josey was nominated to the ALA Council as vice president/president elect in June 1983.[32] His many years of working in the academic arena and his leadership role at the New York State Department of Education, combined with his activism in the profession, aptly prepared him for his role in leading the ALA. "Josey had 'presence' . . . he was an effective president because he presented himself well and was a good public speaker" according to former president of the ALA, Barbara Ford.[33] Ford believes that Josey led from a high moral ground with very strong ideas that were firmly based on the values and principles of the profession. She further contends that "he's a very good listener, open to change, and inclusive in allowing people to have their say; he tries to come to consensus while not compromising his principles."[34] She believes that these qualities were the hallmarks of his exceptional leadership. Because so many members of the association shared the same views about Josey, a movement to elect him as the first African American male president began in the 1980s.

When Josey prepared to take on his new leadership role as the 101st president of the ALA, Ronald Reagan had just been reelected for a second term as president of the United States. President Reagan's second term was marked by the end of the Cold War as well as a number of scandals, notably the Iran-Contra Affair. The president had ordered a massive military buildup in an arms race with the Soviet Union and that took its toll on the already diminishing economy. Thus, many publicly funded institutions, including libraries, suffered from funding and financial cutbacks.

Accordingly, Josey chose "Forging Coalitions for the Public Good" as his presidential theme. He envisioned that libraries could be a public good especially at a time of declining funding for public sector institutions. One of the threats was the growing concern for "alternative" sources of funding for libraries. Another aspect of Josey's public good theme was the growth of

Figure 4.1.   E. J. Josey speaking at a conference, circa 1970. *Courtesy of the*
University of Illinois Archives" ALA0002099

private sector information services and the trend toward commoditization of
information. "Information as a commodity" was a prevailing theme during
the 1980s. The privatization of information services and the belief in neolib-
eral market forces had been encouraged by many, and individuals had begun
to buy into the notion that private sector information services can replace
services offered by public institutions and can do so without expense to the
taxpayer. Josey wanted to dispel this belief by reaffirming the concept of the
public good and developing coalitions with other organizations to promote
public sector support of libraries. His primary objective was to establish
coalitions for effective action that would last over a period of time. He
articulated his vision in his inaugural address on June 27, 1984, in Dallas,
Texas:[35]

> The public good, in an even broader sense of the general welfare, is closely
> related to progress for libraries. In a time of attack on the basic freedoms and
> economic well-being of the most vulnerable sections of populations, profes-
> sional groups must recognize their stake in the outcome of that attack and their
> responsibilities to support the freedoms and welfare of these people. Librarians
> therefore need to integrate their goals with the goals of greatest importance of
> the American people, e.g., the preservation of basic democratic liberties, the
> enlargement of equal opportunity for women and minorities, and the continu-

Figure 4.2.   E. J. Josey speaking at a conference, circa 1970. *Courtesy of the University of Illinois Archives: ALA0002096*

> ance of earlier national planning to raise the level of the educational and
> economic well-being of greater numbers of the population.[36]

Although coalition building was a new concept when Josey started his presidency, today coalitions and partnerships are a vital component within the ALA to advance its goals. A major activity that Josey used to promote his agenda of forging coalitions occurred in his planning for his presidential program. Applying a conference-within-a-conference approach, Josey brought hundreds of leaders in librarianship and related fields together to write and present position papers that served as a catalyst for discussion at the program. Topics included coalition building and the importance of forging those coalitions for the 1980s. His program resonated with many people and he was highly praised for his meticulous organizing and innovative plan to reach outside the profession in order to build alliances with teachers, politicians, and other professionals.[37]

Other examples of Josey's efforts to build coalitions can be seen in his appointment of two key committees. His vision of equality was further carried out in his term by establishing an ALA committee on pay equity. This

Figure 4.3. **Josey as ALA president-elect.** *Courtesy of the University of Illinois Archives: ALA0002097*

committee, which was endorsed by the council as a subcommittee of the Status of Women in Librarianship Committee, had already begun efforts to coordinate local and state groups to strengthen the fight to increase the minimum salaries of librarians to the level of other professionals with comparable graduate degrees. The newly created ad hoc committee, the Coalition on Government Information, comprised of librarians and members from other local and national organizations, was concerned with the continued dissemination and access to vital government information and sought to explore creative approaches to distributing government information to the larger society.[38]

Josey also created a presidential committee on library services to minorities. The findings from the 1984 National Commission on Libraries and Information Science report entitled "Equity at Issue," indicated that there was an underrepresentation of librarians of color in professional positions, set the ALA on a course to promote diversity. The committee was charged with providing a forum to research, monitor, discuss, and address national diversity issues and trends as well as to analyze and address the impact of diversity issues and trends on the profession and the relevance and effectiveness of library leadership, library organizations, and library services to an increasingly diverse society; also, to provide council and ALA membership with information needed for the establishment of ALA policies, actions, and initiatives related to national diversity issues and trends. The very nature of the committee brought about an awareness and change in several organizations, including ALA Council, ALA Divisions, ALA Offices and Units, ALA Round Tables, ALA Committees, and ALA Affiliates.

The committee was known as the Minority for Concerns and Committee on Diversity. Patricia Glass Schuman, former president of the ALA and longtime Josey friend, contends that during his presidency, "he literally changed the color of the Association's committees through his appointments."[39] Sal Guerena also praised Josey for his commitment to librarians of color: "His major Equity at Issue initiative was a broad-based strategy that was all-inclusive and aimed to create systemic change from throughout the ALA organization to create positive change within ALA and achieve greater equity to meet the needs of people of color."[40]

Arguably, the highlight of his term as president was the joint meeting of the BCALA and the Kenya Library Association for a weeklong seminar prior to the International Federation of Library Associations and Institutions (IFLA) Conference in Nairobi, Kenya. Approximately thirty librarians engaged in discussion of issues of mutual concern. Topics that were addressed included building ethnic collections and resources, challenges with publishing and acquiring African and African American materials, and information technology.[41] George Grant, dean of library and information resources at the Dean B. Ellis Library at Arkansas State University, a friend of Josey's for more than four decades and an active member of the BCALA, remembers that "the seminar was hailed as success and participants left with a sense of accomplishment and a vow to combat racism at all levels of librarianship.[42]

PIONEERING INTERNATIONAL RELATIONS WITH LIBRARIANS

Since 1927, the establishment of the IFLA has been instrumental in bringing librarians together from around the world.[43] Recognizing early on that international relations was not a priority for ALA, Josey advocated for the exchange of books and other materials from overseas and Africa.[44] He first became involved with IFLA in 1974 when their meeting was held in Washington, DC. It was the first time that IFLA had met in North America since World War II.[45] Josey had a strong interest in librarians from African countries and firmly believed that international relations could be improved through international librarianship.[46] His contention was:

> We all live in a global village, in which people cannot exist in an isolationist fashion. Whatever happens in Beijing or Moscow, or wherever else in the world, affects everyone. In other words, all nations are increasingly being influenced by the activities of other nations.[47]

Josey became an advocate of international librarianship and urged the ALA to work collaboratively to improve international information transfer.[48] In 1977, when Moon was president of ALA, he appointed Josey as chair of the ALA International Relations Committee (IRC).[49] Although the appointment was a surprise to many people who were unaware of Josey's international interests, he became as prominent on the international arena as he was on the domestic front.

Despite the ALA's long-term interest in international concerns, the association had not developed a formal policy on international relations until Josey chaired the committee in 1977. At that time, he directed a series of hearings that resulted in the adoption of ALA Policy 57.[50] The commitment in the area of international relations is carried out in part through the activities and programs of ALA's International Relations Office. The ALA established objectives and responsibilities that were adopted in 1978 as follows:

1. To encourage the exchange, dissemination, and access to information and the unrestricted flow of library materials in all formats throughout the world.
2. To promote and support human rights and intellectual freedom worldwide.

3. To foster, promote, support, and participate in the development of international standards relating to library and information services, including information tools and technologies.
4. To promote legislation and treaties that will strengthen library, information, and telecommunication services worldwide.
5. To encourage involvement of librarians, information specialists, and other library personnel in international library activities and in the development of solutions to library service problems that span national boundaries.
6. To promote the education of librarians, information specialists, and other library personnel in such ways that they are knowledgeable about librarianship in the international context.
7. To promote public awareness of the importance of the role of librarians, libraries, and information services in national and international development.[51]

Josey chaired the IRC again in 1987–1990 and revised the IRC policy to encourage member library publishers and others to donate materials to libraries in developing countries.[52] As a spokesman against discrimination, it was no surprise when Josey led a campaign against apartheid in South Africa. At the IFLA General Conference held in Chicago in August 1985, Josey vehemently protested against the South African delegation.[53] The impetus for his objection was an excerpt published in the South African newspaper *Cape Argus*, which reported that large numbers of South African public libraries remained closed to blacks.[54] At the conclusion of the opening session, Josey, like he had done many times before, "rose to protest the participation of the twelve South African delegates, whose hands he said were 'dripping with the blood of thousands of innocent people. We know . . . that the [conference] theme, Universal Availability of Information, is meaningless in that troubled land.'"[55]

Josey and his supporters advocated that IFLA exclude South African apartheid associations and institutions as members. During this time there were several community resource centers and soon thereafter an alternative library association; but these kinds of libraries did not have much money and were not likely to try to join IFLA. However, they were not excluded under the resolution that was proposed to the IFLA Council in 1985. At the next IFLA Council meeting, ALA Council member, Norman Horrocks, requested a report on IFLA's inquiry into apartheid in South African libraries. Secretary General Margreet Wijnstroom presented a resolution that was signed by members from Nigeria, Kenya, Senegal, France, Denmark, England, and the United States that read: "South African institutions that adhere to apartheid policies will continue to be denied the privilege of membership in IFLA."[56] Although the resolution passed unanimously and President Else Granheim announced that actions would be taken to monitor the situation in South Africa,[57] very little was done to implement the resolution.

Al Kagan, professor of library administration and African studies bibliographer emeritus at the University of Illinois Library at Urbana-Champaign, and a member of IFLA, was the Social Responsibility Round Table (SRRT) councilor who collaborated with Josey on many issues in IFLA. Kagan recalls the frustration with the conflict with the IFLA Council:

> Every year at IFLA, we would put together an international delegation of course led by E. J., we made an appointment with the IFLA president to ask for the status of implementing that resolution and every year the IFLA president would say that they were doing another study, another survey, another something, and they hadn't done anything with the resolution besides study the problem.[58]

The reluctance of IFLA's council to act on the antiapartheid movement forced Josey and his supporters to hold a demonstration outside of the IFLA meeting in Stockholm, Sweden, in 1990. They joined forces with the local antiapartheid solidarity movement, and, much to the chagrin the IFLA officers, they passed out flyers, made signs and banners, and stood outside the IFLA conference center protesting the council's refusal to enforce the resolution.[59] That same year at the ALA conference in Chicago, the association's position on South Africa was the foremost concern. As the chair of the IRC, Josey "held hearings to determine whether ALA should endorse the American Association of Publishers (AAP) Report."[60] The report entitled "The Starvation of Young Black Minds: The Effects of Book Boycotts in South Africa," written by notable African American librarians Robert Wedgeworth and Lisa Drew, "proposed lifting the boycott on books."[61] However, many of the members of the ALA did not want to lift the ban. Josey fervently supported the ban because he believed the great majority of the South African population would never have access to the books under apartheid. Moreover, there were very few libraries in the townships or in the rural areas that would benefit from the books.[62]

During one of the IRC hearings, Wedgeworth, having just returned from a trip to South Africa sponsored by the AAP, opposed the ALA taking a position to boycott South Africa and wanted to keep selling books to South Africa. Therefore, "when E. J. had the hearing, he [Wedgeworth] was the first speaker at the microphone and blasted the policy and then stormed out of the room. . . . Every other speaker at the hearing supported the policy of boycotting South Africa, Wedgeworth was the only one who did not."[63]

The boycott on books was the hottest issue to be debated at the conference in years. It was fervently argued, not only on the floor of council but also during membership and executive board meetings.[64] The controversy over apartheid further illuminated the chasm that existed between Wedgeworth and Josey. It was well known that these two highly regarded leaders did not agree on many issues and did not get along, mainly because of their ideological differences. Furthermore, Wedgeworth was bound by his position as the executive director (1972–1985) of the ALA. An official of the ALA, he could not be affiliated with organizations like the Black Caucus, of which he was a member for two years.[65] He and Josey often found themselves on the opposite side of issues—Josey clearly articulating what he believed was right for his constituency and Wedgeworth working on behalf of the general body of members. Interestingly, when examining Josey's personal papers, there was much correspondence between him and Wedgeworth. There was no glaring evidence of disharmony between the two, which may speak to the fact that regardless of the differing philosophical views, they held each other in mutual respect.

THE BLACK CAUCUS OF ALA

Parallel institutions created by black professionals during the 1970s promoted a consciousness that challenged the dominant culture's ideology on the role of marginalized people in professional organizations. Prior to the civil rights movement, black professionals often accepted an inferior status in the workplace, which included facing discrimination in applying for management positions. In the aftermath of the civil rights movement, many African American professionals separated from their professional organizations to form associations where they could maintain themselves and ensure the survival of the greater black community.[66] Organizations such as the National Association of Black Social Workers, the National Conference of Black Lawyers, and the National Council of Black Political Scientists are examples of how African American professionals parted ways with their parent institutions to have greater control over their professional destinies.[67] Contrarily, other African American professionals like librarians maneuvered within their institutional structures and formed affiliate organizations. These organizations allowed them to promote leadership within their parent organizations.

A popular approach used to combat discrimination in professional organizations occurred through the formation of caucuses. In the early 1970s, blacks in the US Congress became frustrated with President Nixon administration's reluctance to address the needs of African Americans and established the Congressional Black Caucus.[68] African American librarians adopted this same premise and formed the BCALA. In librarianship in general, and in the ALA in particular, black librarians found that BCALA allowed them to work within the framework of the parent organization to fight against the injustice they experienced at work and in the ALA. The BCALA has played a major role in the ALA through its leadership and its ability to influence policy affecting people of color. Moreover, successful efforts to recruit African Americans to become librarians are a means of cultivating future leaders in the ALA. The Black Caucus' story mirrors the broader movement by black professionals in organizations in the aftermath of the civil rights movement.

Advocacy for equity in the ALA during the civil rights movement played a major role in confronting the color line in the association during the 1970s. Drawing strength from his earlier experience fighting for change in the organization during the height of the civil rights movement, Josey was uniquely positioned to lead a delegation of black librarians to form a caucus. By late 1970, a small group of black and white librarians, who met at the midwinter meetings, agreed to establish the BCALA as a major activist organization within the ALA.[69] Considered by many as the moral conscience of the American Library Association, the caucus members were invigorated by changing times, and through this new organization they were now capable of influencing the larger community.

Although the BCALA was officially established in 1970,[70] the momentum for the collaboration began in the 1930s and 1940s when a small number of African American librarians who attended the ALA conferences would assemble in hotel suites to commiserate about the injustices they experienced.[71] Black librarians would also come together "when the School of Library Service of Atlanta University began to sponsor alumni dinners."[72] Most African American librarians attended regardless of whether they were graduates of the school or not because they found value in the support from fellow African American librarians.[73]

Under the suggestion of Effie Lee Morris, black librarians met at the 1968 Annual Conference to discuss their concerns about not having a voice in the ALA. However, it was not until two years later that the group formally came together as a governing body. Out of that meeting, it was decided that there was a need for the creation of a formal organization. In 1969, Josey was a member of the ALA presidential nominating committee. In this role he wanted to find qualified black candidates and socially responsible white contenders to run for members of council in the next election. Therefore, he sent letters inviting all African American librarians to attend the 1970 midwinter meeting to discuss potential candidates. During the meeting, Josey not only asked for their support for potential council representatives, but he also convinced the group that it was time to elect a black president. They agreed to support notable African American librarian A. P. Marshall for president.[74] Marshall's daughter, Satia Orange, who is a former director of the ALA's Office for Literacy and Outreach Services, recalls that "E. J. was very vocal about issues that were related specifically to racism in the profession."[75] She also believed that Josey, like other African American leaders of his day, rose to prominence because there was a dearth of black leadership.[76] Orange contends that this same need led to the formation of the Black Caucus. She says that "E. J. was very vocal about issues that were related specifically to racism in the profession and that it was a time that led up to a need for the formation of the Black Caucus."[77] Moreover, she adds, "There was a need to pull us together and Josey convened a meeting and it was from that discussion that BCALA was founded."[78]

Morris was a pioneering children's services librarian in the country and an original member of the BCALA. She recalls that Josey's rise to leadership in the ALA "was a period of energy and great excitement."[79] However, she also notes that not all African American librarians were excited about the establishment of a caucus of black librarians. "Many of them were concerned with the progress that had already been made with civil rights and did not want to disturb the status quo."[80]

Establishing a sense of urgency is crucial in garnering cooperation among individuals when working toward organizational change.[81] Although the nation passed the Civil Rights Act of 1964, which legally ended discrimination on the basis of race, the mind-set toward blacks was slow to change. During this time, the ALA leadership appeared insensitive to the injustice African American librarians experienced. The 1970s brought along with it a period of unrest as the Vietnam War raged on, and the internal war against the Black Liberation Movement continued unabated. Issues of empowerment and self-determination were widespread throughout the black community as a whole. No longer were African Americans content to wait for continued progress and change. They were empowered to have a transformation in their profession, and they were determined to have it.

According to many activist librarians, change needed to occur in society. Complacency was no longer tolerated. It was a time when blacks found creative ways to have a voice. In the professional realm, this was accomplished by banding together for a common cause to bring about change. The sense of urgency that was felt by librarians was also felt by blacks in other sectors of society. African Americans wanted civil rights—they wanted to have the same opportunities that whites had in the United States. For the BCALA, the sense of urgency was widely felt among black librarians who were disgruntled by the ALA's lack of responsiveness to address issues of continued discrimination. Moreover, leaders in the ALA were also not sure how to deal with segregation and discrimination. The BCALA believed that one way to make their presence known was to form an organization and try to formulate and implement policies in the ALA that would impact African American librarians. The need for collective response is evident in the words of Robert Wedgeworth:

> Certain events of the past decade indicate a general decline of confidence in
> the integrity of our society. The assassination of Dr. Martin Luther King,

followed by the general rejection of the major findings of the Kerner Commission Report. . . . The significance of these latter events lies in the demand by the non-establishment group to share decision-making powers. [82]

Collective response of an activist community is the rationale for the existence of the Black Caucus; this point is underscored in the preamble to the BCALA constitution:

Whereas, there exists a critical lag in development of librarianship for Blacks, and

Whereas, there are inadequate outlets for the studies and reports dealing with issues relating to Black American citizens, and

Whereas, the library profession in general and the American Library Association (ALA) in particular have been slow in responding to the problems of Black people.

Therefore, we the Black members of the American Library Association have banded together to form this organization. [83]

A fueled sense of urgency throughout BCALA in the 1970s enabled black librarians to take control of their destinies by exhibiting a united front to the executive board of the ALA and calling for action on policies. This fostered a sense of camaraderie and confidence within their organization.

Founded in 1970, the BCALA's mission was to eradicate discrimination that overwhelmed African American librarians in the workplace and in their professional organization. Because of this network of black librarians, aided by the support of other socially responsive professionals in the SRRT, the BCALA was in a unique position to influence policy and advocate change in the library profession. [84] It can be argued that the formation of the BCALA established a pattern of behavior that created a paradigm shift that resulted in transformative attitudes toward African American librarians in the ALA. Generally, the BCALA began to be looked to as a collective voice on policies related to blacks.

Josey was elected as the first chairman of the BCALA, [85] and a statement was delivered at a meeting in 1970 announcing the establishment of the Black Caucus:

As black librarians we are intensely interested in the development of our professional association and our profession; therefore, a committee of the Black Librarians' Caucus has been charged with the responsibility of preparing a program of action. The Black Caucus will continue to meet at the American Library Association conferences for the purpose of evaluating progress being made by the Association in fulfilling its social and professional responsibilities to minority groups in this profession and in the nation. [86]

While major transformations are often associated with one highly visible individual, it typically takes a team of individuals, a coalition of people with the same vision to create change in organizations. However, "no one individual, even a monarch-like CEO, is ever able to develop the right vision, communicate it to large numbers of people, eliminate all the key obstacles, generate short-term wins, lead and manage a dozen of change projects, and anchor new approaches deep in the organization's culture."[87] Essentially, it took great strides by many to bring forth significant changes within the ALA. Transformational leadership is where leaders are agents of change.[88] These leaders develop a vision for the organization, inspire and collectively bond the employees to that vision, and give them a "can do" attitude that makes the vision achievable.

The purpose of the Black Caucus was outlined in a statement of concern. This represented the legitimate concerns of black librarians at the time and continues to influence the goals of the Black Caucus today:

1. To call to the attention of the American Library Association the need to respond positively on behalf of the Black members of the profession and the information needs of the Black community. The Caucus will review, analyze, evaluate, and recommend actions on the needs of Black librarians which will influence their status in the areas of re-

Figure 4.4.   Josey at Black Caucus meeting. *Courtesy of the University of Illinois Archives: ALA0003436*

cruitment, development, advancement and general working conditions.

2. To review the records and evaluate the positions of candidates for the various offices within the ALA to determine their potential impact upon Black librarians and services to the Black community.
3. To actively participate in the activities of the Divisions, Roundtables, and Committees of the American Library Association by active participation within these groups to make sure that they are meeting the needs of the Black librarians.
4. To serve as a clearinghouse for Black librarians in promoting wider participation by Black librarians at all levels of the profession and Association.
5. To support and promote efforts to achieve meaningful communication and equitable representation in state library associations and on the governing and advisory boards of libraries at the state and local levels.
6. To facilitate library service that meets the informational needs of Black people.
7. To encourage the development of authoritative information resources about Black people and the dissemination of this information to the larger community.
8. To open up channels of communication to and through Black librarians in every entity of the American Library Association.[89]

The statement above sheds light on the vision of BCALA. The mission and goals of the association state that BCALA seeks to support the professional needs of African American librarians as well as other minorities.[90] BCALA has also fought against discriminatory practices in libraries as well.

With the announcement of the founding of the BCALA, the effectiveness of the organization was almost immediately tested. Virginia Lacy Jones, dean of the School of Library Service, Atlanta University, introduced a resolution against supporting primary and secondary schools that were created to avoid the 1954 Supreme Court decision. The declaration also stated: "Be it resolved that the libraries and/or librarians who do in fact, through either services or materials, support any such racist institutions be censured by the American Library Association."[91] The bone of contention was the continued lending of materials to and support of these institutions. Although the ALA Council eventually passed the resolution, it was not without much debate.

The mission and goals of the Black Caucus provide a viable model that has been emulated by other ethnic caucuses. State affiliates, such as the California Librarians Black Caucus, have modeled their organizations after BCALA. The latter group raises money for fellowships and supports the recruitment and mentoring of black library students. Josey was also a mentor and supporter of other minorities and encouraged them to start organizations

specifically targeted to their unique needs. It is important to note that after
the Black Caucus was established in 1970, it was not long before other
caucuses were founded. REFORMA, the national association to promote
library and information services to Latinos and the Spanish-speaking, was
founded in 1971. In subsequent years, the Chinese American Librarians Association (1973), the American Indian Library Association (1979), and the
Asian/Pacific Librarians Association (1980) were established.

Josey mentored Sal Guerena, director of the California Ethnic and Multicultural Archives, Department of Special Collections, Donald C. Davidson
Library at the University of California Santa Barbara, and a member of
REFORMA. Guerena often consulted with Josey for advice while working
on the ALA Council. "I sought support and advice for my own initiatives and
those of REFORMA. While serving on ALA Council, I knew I could count
on E. J.'s support and he would speak up forcefully at the microphone whenever I needed another voice for some measure being voted on by Council."[92]

Although BCALA and these other ethnic organizations work closely with
ALA and attempt to influence its policies, they all have the status of independent organizations and are not units of ALA like the SRRT or the Ethnic and
Multicultural Information Exchange Round Table. Starting in 1992, the
BCALA began to organize its own national conferences on a biennial basis,
as well as meeting during the ALA conference. Josey was very much involved with these conferences early on. As the program chair for the first
conference, held in Columbus, Ohio, Orange, director of the ALA's Office
for Literacy and Outreach Services, specifically remembers making special
accommodations for Josey as a speaker and as a person of significance to the
organization.[93] Because of his important role in founding the BCALA and
his contribution to the organization, two scholarships are awarded in his
name annually to African American students enrolled in an ALA accredited
LIS program.

Idealized influence, as conceptualized by Bass, contends that a leader
shows conviction with his or her vision, remains loyal, and is willing to be
put in the line of fire to achieve their goals. Josey demonstrated this when he
successfully proposed that Southern library chapters should be denied full
membership with ALA unless they opened membership to everyone. Other
examples of idealized influence can be seen when he advocated against libraries sending materials to South Africa because of their racist policies.
Josey also demonstrated *inspiration by a leader,* where the leader uses charisma to move the group forward. This is exemplified through his ability to
galvanize people together. Examples of this are seen in the formation of the
BCALA, his election to presidency of the ALA, and his presidential platform
of forging coalitions. Josey's rise to leadership and activism in the profession
began with the historic resolution, peaked when he was elected ALA president in 1984–1985, and culminated when he retired in 1995. He would con-

tinue to remain an influential actor on civil rights long after his retirement with his speaking engagements and publications.

NOTES

1. American Library Association, "About ALA," accessed June 13, 2019, http://www.ala.org/aboutala/.

2. Wayne A. Wiegand, *The Politics of an Emerging Profession: The American Library Association, 1876–1917* (New York: Greenwood Press, 1986), ix.

3. Claud Anderson, *Black Labor, White Wealth: The Search for Power and Economic Justice* (Edgewood, MD: Duncan & Duncan, 1994), 31.

4. American Library Association, "Library Bill of Rights," adopted June 19, 1939, last amended January 29, 2019, http://www.ala.org/advocacy/intfreedom/librarybill.

5. C. B. Roden, "Report of the Committee on Racial Discrimination," *Bulletin of the American Library Association* 31, no. 1 (January 1937): 38; *see* Virginia Lacy Jones, "A Dean's Career," in *The Black Librarian in America*, ed. E. J. Josey (Metuchen, NJ: Scarecrow Press, 1970), 26; Casper LeRoy Jordan and E. J. Josey, "A Chronology of Events in Black Librarianship," in *Handbook of Black Librarianship*, ed. E. J. Josey and Marva L. DeLoach, 2nd ed. (Lanham, MD: Scarecrow Press, 2000), 7; Lorna Peterson, "Alternative Perspectives in Library and Information Science: Issues of Race," *Journal of Education for Library and Information Science* 37, no. 2 (Spring 1996): 169–70, https://www.jstor.org/stable/40324271; Dennis Thomison, *A History of the American Library Association, 1876–1972* (Chicago: American Library Association, 1978), 130–32.

6. Jones, "Dean's Career," 39.

7. E. J. Josey, "A Dreamer—with a Tiny Spark, in *The Black Librarian in America*, ed. E. J. Josey (Metuchen, NJ: Scarecrow Press, 1970), 300, 313.

8. Thomas Lawrence King, "Support for Human Rights in Librarianship: The Legacy of E. J. Josey," in *E. J. Josey: An Activist Librarian*, ed. Ismail Abdullahi (Metuchen, NJ: Scarecrow Press, 1992), 96.

9. E. J. Josey, in personal communication with the author, March 7, 2001.

10. Josey, "Dreamer," 311.

11. Eric Moon, "A 'Chapter' Chapter: E. J., ALA, and Civil Rights," in *E. J. Josey: An Activist Librarian*, ed. Ismail Abdullahi (Metuchen, NJ: Scarecrow Press, 1992), 44.

12. "Segregation and ALA Membership," *Wilson Library Bulletin* 36, no. 7 (March 1962): 558–61, 579.

13. Josey, "Dreamer," 313.

14. Civil Rights Act of 1964, Pub. L. No. 88–352, 78 Stat. 241.

15. Josey, "Dreamer," 313.

16. Josey, "Dreamer," 314.

17. Josey, in personal communication with the author, March 7, 2001.

18. Josey, "Dreamer," 314.

19. "Memo to Members," *ALA Bulletin* 50, no. 7 (July–August 1964): 592, https://www.jstor.org/stable/i25696961; *see* Casper LeRoy Jordan and E. J. Josey, "A Chronology of Events in Black Librarianship," in *Handbook of Black Librarianship*, ed. E. J. Josey and Ann Allen Shockley (Littleton, CO: Libraries Unlimited, 1977), 20.

20. Josey, "Dreamer," 316.

21. Josey, in personal communication with the author, March 7, 2001.

22. Jordan and Josey, "Chronology of Events in Black Librarianship," 20; Josey, "Dreamer," 316–17; King, "Support for Human Rights in Librarianship," 96; John Mark Tucker, ed., *Untold Stories: Civil Rights, Libraries, and Black Librarianship* (Champaign: University of Illinois Graduate School of Library and Information Science, 1998), 120–21.

23. Clara Stanton Jones, "E. J. Josey: Librarian for All Seasons," in *E. J. Josey: An Activist Librarian*, ed. Ismail Abdullahi (Metuchen, NJ: Scarecrow Press, 1992), 12.

24. Jones, "E. J. Josey," 13.

25. Jones, "E. J. Josey," 13.

26. Jones, "E. J. Josey," 15.

27. Kathleen Weibel, personal interview with the author, April 9, 2007; *see* C. S. Jones, "E. J. Josey," 15–16.

28. Jones, "E. J. Josey," 13–18.

29. Sanford Berman, in personal communication with the author, April 26, 2007.

30. Steven A. Knowlton, "Three Decades since *Prejudices and Antipathies*: A Study of Changes in the Library of Congress Subject Headings," *Cataloging and Classification Quarterly* 40, no. 2 (2005): 125, 127–28, https://doi.org/10.1300/J104v40n02_08.

31. Berman, in personal communication with the author, April 26, 2007.

32. Lucille Thomas, "E. J. Josey, the 101st President of the American Library Association," in *E. J. Josey: An Activist Librarian*, ed. Ismail Abdullahi (Metuchen, NJ: Scarecrow Press, 1992), 21.

33. Barbara Ford, in personal communication with the author, April 9, 2007.

34. Ford, in personal communication with the author, April 9, 2007.

35. Thomas, "E. J. Josey," 23.

36. Patricia Glass Schuman, "E. J. Josey as Mentor and Leader in ALA," in *E. J. Josey: An Activist Librarian*, ed. Ismail Abdullahi (Metuchen, NJ: Scarecrow Press, 1992), 31.

37. Thomas, "E. J. Josey," 21–24.

38. Schuman, "E. J. Josey as Mentor and Leader in ALA," 29.

39. Schuman, "E. J. Josey as Mentor and Leader in ALA, 29.

40. Sal Guerena, in personal communication with the author, September 10, 2007.

41. Marva L. DeLoach, "An African Odyssey," *Library Journal* 110, no. 4 (March 1985): 57–62.

42. George Grant, in personal communication with the author, October 12, 2007.

43. Ching-chih Chen, "International Relations: The Role of an Individual," in *E. J. Josey: An Activist Librarian*, ed. Ismail Abdullahi (Metuchen, NJ: Scarecrow Press, 1992), 176.

44. Chen, "International Relations," 178–79.

45. Chen, "International Relations," 176.

46. Chen, "International Relations," 177.

47. E. J. Josey, in personal communication with the author, March 10, 2001.

48. Chen, "International Relations," 177–79.

49. Chen, "International Relations," 177.

50. Chen, "International Relations," 177–78.

51. Vivian D. Hewitt, "An Internationalist in ALA and IFLA," in *E. J. Josey: An Activist Librarian*, ed. Ismail Abdullahi (Metuchen, NJ: Scarecrow Press, 1992), 187–88.

52. Chen, "International Relations," 177–78.

53. "Sleep No More at IFLA: Report on the International Federation of Library Associations & Institutions 51st Council and General Conference, August 18–24, Chicago, U.S.A.," *American Libraries* 16, no. 9 (October 1985): 610, https://www.jstor.org/stable/25629740.

54. "Notes and Asides at an International Conference," *American Libraries* 16, no. 9 (October 1985): 615, https://www.jstor.org/stable/25629740.

55. Hewitt, "An Internationalist in ALA and IFLA," 189 (brackets in original).

56. Hewitt, "An Internationalist in ALA and IFLA," 189.

57. Hewitt, "An Internationalist in ALA and IFLA," 189–90.

58. Al Kagan, personal interview with the author, April 9, 2007.

59. Kagan, personal interview with the author, April 9, 2007.

60. Hewitt, "An Internationalist in ALA and IFLA," 190.

61. Hewitt, "An Internationalist in ALA and IFLA," 190.

62. Hewitt, "An Internationalist in ALA and IFLA," 191–92

63. Kagan, personal interview with the author, April 9, 2007.

64. Hewitt, "An Internationalist in ALA and IFLA," 190–91.

65. Robert Wedgeworth, in personal communication with the author, February 23, 2006.

66. Darlene Clark Hine, "Black Professionals and Race Consciousness: Origins of the Civil Rights Movement, 1890–1950," *The Journal of American History* 89, no. 4 (March 2003): 1279–94, https://www.jstor.org/stable/3092543.

67. E. J. Josey, "Black Caucus of the American Library Association," in *Handbook of Black Librarianship*, ed. E. J. Josey and Ann Allen Shockley (Littleton, CO: Libraries Unlimited, 1977), 66.

68. Josey, "Black Caucus of the American Library Association," 66–67.

69. Josey, "Black Caucus of the American Library Association," 68–69.

70. Black Caucus of the American Library Association, "Our History," accessed December 20, 2018, https://www.bcala.org/.

71. Josey, "Black Caucus of the American Library Association," 67.

72. Josey, "Black Caucus of the American Library Association," 67.

73. Josey, "Black Caucus of the American Library Association," 67.

74. E. J. Josey, personal interview with the author, April 10, 2007.

75. Satia Orange, in personal communication with author, September 13, 2007.

76. Orange, in personal communication with the author, September 13, 2007.

77. Orange, in personal communication with the author, September 13, 2007.

78. Orange, in personal communication with the author, September 13, 2007.

79. Effie Lee Morris, in personal communication with the author, July 31, 2007.

80. Morris, in personal communication with the author, July 31, 2007.

81. John P. Kotter, *Leading Change* (Boston, MA: Harvard Business Review Press, 2012), 37–38.

82. Robert Wedgeworth, "ALA and the Black Librarian: Strategies for the '70's," in *Black Librarian in America*, ed. E. J. Josey (Metuchen, NJ: Scarecrow Press, 1970), 69.

83. Constitution and Bylaws of the Black Caucus of the American Library Association, January 21, 1970, amended 2017, https://www.bcala.org/bylaws/.

84. Josey, "Black Caucus of the American Library Association," 67–68.

85. Josey, "Black Caucus of the American Library Association," 67.

86. Josey, "Black Caucus of the American Library Association," 69.

87. Kotter, *Leading Change*, 53.

88. Steven L. McShane and May Ann Von Glinow, *Organizational Behavior: Emerging Knowledge and Practice for the Real World*, 5th ed. (Boston, MA: McGraw-Hill/Irwin, 2010), 371–75.

89. Constitution and Bylaws of the Black Caucus of the American Library Association.

90. Black Caucus of the American Library Association, "Our History."

91. Josey, "Dreamer," 318.

92. Guerena, in personal communication with the author, September 10, 2007.

93. Orange, in personal communication with the author, September 13, 2007.

Chapter Five

A Model for Leadership in LIS

In early 2019, the Association for Library and Information Science Education (ALISE) held a leadership academy to allow its members opportunities to explore their interest in seeking leadership positions as deans, directors, or program chairs within departments and schools of LIS.[1] This stands as evidence that leadership has always been important. Leadership has been a longstanding interest in LIS education in an effort to "gain an understanding of how change can be effectively and appropriately managed."[2] That is why E. J. Josey's legacy stands as a model for twenty-first-century leadership in LIS.

LEADERSHIP IN LIS EDUCATION

Although growth and change are inevitable in any organization, including LIS, transformational leadership can inspire and motivate LIS professionals to innovate and create change that will help develop and shape the future of the profession. In fact, the ALA's Presidential Task Force on Library Education added "principled, transformational leadership" to its Core Competences for Librarianship in 2009.[3] While it is unclear how the ALA defines "principled" in relation to transformational leadership,[4] there is agreement that principled transformational leadership combines ethical and moral principles with the tenets of idealized influence, intellectual stimulation, individual consideration, and inspirational motivation described by Bass.[5]

In many ways, not only did Josey embody transformational leadership as an LIS professional and educator, he also possessed a high degree of ethics and morality. Many would agree that he set a precedent for others to aspire to through his teaching, scholarship, and service. Josey's impact on LIS education is enduring. One way to fully understand how his leadership was trans-formative is to explore the history of LIS education.

HISTORY OF LIS EDUCATION

Students of early LIS education were trained under the British apprenticeship system common in the late eighteenth to early nineteenth centuries. Howev-er, with industrialization of the 1800s, this very specialized method of train-ing quickly became ineffective to prepare librarians for the workforce across the United States.[6] The dismantling of the British system created an opportu-nity for a new method of training. One of the most prominent leaders in developing librarianship as a profession was Melvil Dewey. After his devel-opment of the Dewey Decimal System during his tenure at Amherst College, he founded the ALA in 1876. The creation of a professional organization for librarians prompted the creation of the first library school. The Columbia School of Library Economy opened in January 1887 with three men and seventeen women as its first class. Training was for three months, with an internship that lasted up to two years. The school later moved to the New York State Library in Albany after Columbia trustees disagreed with Dewey's inclusion of women in his courses. It was in Albany, where Dewey's vice director, Mary Salome Cutler Fairchild, added theoretical and cultural aspects of librarianship to what had been a very practical curricu-lum.[7]

Due to the success of this program, three additional library schools opened by 1900: Pratt Institute, Drexel University, and the Armour Institute (which became the library school at the University of Illinois in 1897).[8] Each school made unique contributions to the field: Pratt established the first chil-dren's librarianship specialization; Drexel's director published the first major texts on reference materials and book selection; and the Armour Institute developed its program into a four-year bachelor's degree.[9] By 1919, there were fifteen library programs, most of which awarded a fifth-year bachelor of library science degree after four years of undergraduate education.[10] At this time, the master's in library science (MLS) was only awarded at the predecessor institution to the State University of New York at Albany in Albany, New York.[11] Tensions developed between the ALA and the schools, so the library schools formed their own association, the Association of American Library Schools (AALS), in 1916. AALS changed its name to the Association for Library and Information Science Education in 1983.[12]

The Carnegie Corporation conducted a review of its libraries and found that they had inadequate resources and training, and thus they ordered a study on LIS education with particular focus on library schools. The 1923 William-son Report (headed by Charles C. Williamson) strongly influenced the direction of LIS education. The report recommended librarian training as not simply training, but a professional degree best combined with a college education.[13] In 1926, the graduate library school at the University of Chicago created the first doctoral program in "library science" and, by 1950, most library schools offered the MLS.[14] The Carnegie Corporation wanted to encourage library services to blacks in the South, so they established a grant to open the Hampton Institute Library School in 1925. It was the first and only school to offer a bachelor's degree in library science accredited by the board of education for librarianship and the ALA.[15]

The decision to open a library school specifically for blacks in the south was highly controversial and was heavily debated by citizens interested in librarianship in the South.[16] Unfortunately, the library school closed in 1939 due to lack of funding,[17] but it reopened two years later at Atlanta University. In total, there were five HBCU library schools: Hampton University (1925–1954), Alabama A&M University (1969–1982), the University of the District of Columbia (1969–1979), Clark Atlanta University (1939–2005), and North Carolina Central University (NCCU) (1941), the sole remaining library school at an HBCU. Josey made significant contributions to NCCU. He acted in an advisory role from 1970 until his retirement in 1995 by serving on the school's advisory council.[18] In this capacity, he suggested potential research and publishing areas for faculty research; he worked closely with the deans of the school on student recruitment; and he enhanced their black librarians collection.[19] Former dean of the school, Benjamin Speller, asserts:

> E. J. Josey has been a true friend of North Carolina Central University. The NCCU School of Library and Information Sciences has benefitted from his leadership and wisdom as a trusted advisor to two deans. He has provided significant support of the faculty's research productivity. He has served as a mentor for students he directed to the school. . . . Through E. J. Josey's coaching, nurturing, and mentorship, a prominent and permanent place for Americans of African descent has been ensured in the profession of librarianship and in American society.[20]

Librarians who came from these programs "have had the leading role in educating Black professionals to pursue careers in librarianship and leadership positions. Together, library educators and librarians have pioneered and persisted in achieving access to, and participation in, professional organizations. They have served as mentors and role models for many individuals and have contributed to the scholarly record of librarianship."[21]

The first negro library conference "was held in the Museum of Hampton Institute (now Hampton University) on March 15–18, 1927."[22] It was organized by Hampton Institute alumnus Thomas Fountain Blue, who became director of the Louisville Free Libraries Colored branches. The conference was sponsored by the Carnegie Corporation and attended by more than forty librarians from the South. [23] Hampton also produced notable graduates like Virginia Lacy Jones.

The ALA Board of Education for Librarianship issued standards that required the graduate master's degree as the educational standard in 1951. Five years later, it formed the ALA Committee on Accreditation, which disbanded other forms of library education besides the graduate schools. [24] In August 2018, Hampton University held a forum on minority recruitment and retention in the library and information science profession. The goal of the conference was to address the crucial issue of diversity and inclusion of minority librarians. [25]

Although the 1960s was a time of social and political upheaval in the United States, the decade proved to be a period of growth for library science education. The economic expansion and the availability of federal funds offered a need for more libraries and professionally trained librarians to staff them. [26] It was also in the 1960s when library science programs began to add the term "information science" to their names. The first school to do this was at the University of Pittsburgh in 1964. [27] By the 1970s, there were more than seventy ALA-accredited programs in the United States and Canada. Over the next few decades, the numbers declined significantly largely due to a confluence of factors that included an economic downturn, the ubiquity of technology, low campus profiles that resulted in funding shortages, and the development of online education. [28] At the turn of the century, the number of programs plummeted to fifty-six. [29] Not only was there a closure of library schools (HBCUs and others), there was also a merger of library programs with other disciplines on university campuses. Scholars like Michael K. Buckland began to question what is information science and, more specifically, what is information? [30]

Today, the LIS curriculum is constantly under development, and the MLIS in its current form was not always in consensus on the standard for the profession. The traditional roles of library and information professionals were no longer adequate to support the changed environment. At the turn of the twenty-first century, focus on information and the rapid development of digital information led to the creation of the information school (iSchool). The idea for the iSchool originated in 1998 when informal discussions about the impact of changing technology on LIS were held among the deans from the School of Information Sciences at the University of Pittsburgh (Toni Carbo), Syracuse University School of Information Studies (Donald Marchand), Drexel University College of Information Science and Technology (Richard Lytle)—the self-proclaimed "Gang of Three"—and later "The Gang of Four" when the dean of the School of Communication, Information and Library Studies at Rutgers University (Richard Budd) joined the group. [31]

As of 2018, there were more than one hundred member iSchools world-wide.[32]

The iSchools organization was founded in 2005 by a collective of information schools.[33] Not only had LIS seen a dramatic shift in the traditional roles of librarians and information professionals, the changing demographics of the nation, and the social issues that had a tremendous impact on the profession, but it was technology that has had the most catalyzing effect on the profession. These are the goals of the iSchool:

1. Lead and promote the information field. Member schools are committed to collective efforts that will shape the information field, communicate its purpose and value, and enhance its visibility.
2. Create effective responses to strategic research and academic opportunities. Member schools work together to enhance academic initiatives and to leverage funding for important research challenges in the information field.
3. Provide support for, and solutions to, shared challenges. Member schools provide one another with mutual support and a collective identity, helping constituent schools respond to local challenges, and advance the information field.
4. Provide informed perspectives on matters of public policy as they affect the collection, organization, dissemination, use, and preservation of information.[34]

Traditional challenges that impact the LIS profession, such as information access, equity of information, privacy, First Amendment rights, and information literacy, are the same issues that the profession grappled with in the twentieth century. They have been exacerbated in this new technologically driven climate. We live in a time where we have information warfare and the need for information warriors—defenders of information fluency. Thus, a new kind of leadership with a new set of skills and orientation is needed in the profession. The educational standards for librarians and information professionals will continue to develop as the needs of the society evolves. These challenges are related to not adequately arming people with the skills that are needed to thrive in today's information-centric society. In essence, these are social justice concerns—many of the same issues that Josey advocated. Perhaps we can learn from his innovative thinking and out-of-the-box methods that made him successful in his teaching, scholarship, and service.

TEACHING

Thirty-three years after accepting his first job at the Free Library of Philadelphia, Josey embarked on a teaching career at the University of Pittsburgh School of Library Science. Josey's return to academia after working for the New York State Department of Education for twenty years was the fulfillment of his earliest ambition to become a teacher by becoming a library educator.[35] He had already been recognized as a researcher and had published several notable works. He was recruited to the University of Pittsburgh by provost Donald Henderson, who at the time was the acting director of Pittsburgh's library system. Josey was ambivalent about leaving New York, similar to the feelings that he had when he left Savannah State College, because he enjoyed his job and the work that he was doing as president of the Albany chapter of the NAACP. After completing his term as president of the ALA in 1986, Josey accepted a position as senior professor at the University of Pittsburgh School of Library and Information Science (SLIS). In a memorandum to the faculty and staff at the University of Pittsburgh SLIS, interim dean, Allen Kent, issued this announcement:

> E. J. Josey's expert knowledge of all types of libraries, of the capabilities and logistics of sharing resources and services, of administration, funding, graduate and continuing education will contribute greatly to course and curriculum development and professional awareness of students and faculty. His example will suggest admirable goals of professional development including research and publication as well as teaching.[36]

His new role as professor of LIS allowed him to continue his advocacy on human and civil rights. Josey had been a lifelong promoter of librarianship to many he encountered; however, it was not until he came to the University of Pittsburgh that he was able to instill in his students the fervor for equality for all and a passion for library science. Perhaps this is why so many of his students have been highly involved in the ALA and are indebted to him for the guidance and support they received. Through his teaching, he mentored and molded numerous students. He used his scholarship not only to advance his beliefs but also as a means of offering publishing opportunities to students who may not have had the chance otherwise. As a statesman in the LIS profession, Josey is only matched by his desire to mentor those who had a shared enthusiasm for justice. Accordingly, many colleagues of Josey echoed those sentiments. "I think his greatest contribution is his keen insight on human and social justice and his recruitment of minorities to the profession."[37]

Academia has enticed many African Americans because of their desire to learn the tools that will allow them to wage ideological struggle for the hearts and minds of black people in particular, and humanity in general, in order to collectively pursue a more positive direction that will result in better lives for all. Given Josey's extraordinary lived experiences, it was no surprise that he pursued a career in academia. In earlier chapters, we have seen that education has been a recurring theme throughout his life. From the time he attended I. C. Norcom High School, where he excelled in his subjects, until his retirement from the University of Pittsburgh and beyond, he had been an infallible advocate for education. This is exemplified through the countless students, particularly African Americans, he recruited and mentored over the years, as well as the voluminous publications as a result of the research and service he provided to the universities where he worked and the profession.

In his role as professor of library science, Josey brought many of his ideas about equity and diversity into the classroom. Courses that he taught included libraries and society, academic library management, and library service to special populations, and courses that he designed, such as library services for the underserved and library services for the aging. When asked about the courses that he enjoyed teaching the most, Josey responded, "Well . . . the core courses, the major foundations course, and the librarianship in society. I enjoyed those courses because they had so many philosophical underpinnings from ALA that I tried to inculcate to the students. . . . I also tried to revive some history of librarianship."[38] As one former student noted about Josey:

> Reviewing my notes of his lectures I was surprised and impressed by the scope of the material covered, the wealth of detail, the seminal nature of the suggested readings; but these are only incidental to the spirit of the man himself. A few phrases, a few quotes, a few principles infinitely rich in their suggestiveness—these are things that I internalized on the spot. They made me think, provided me with guidance, clarified the challenges ahead. These are the things not to be scribbled on a yellow legal pad; they are meant to touch and awaken the individual's sense of mission.[39]

Toni Carbo Bearman, who was hired as the SLIS dean when Josey joined the faculty, recalls that "[s]tudents sp[oke] highly of his knowledge, his exceptional communication skills, and his concern for them as individuals."[40] Bearman and Josey knew each other for several years prior to working together at Pittsburgh. Their association began in the early 1970s when they both worked on the National Commission on Libraries and Information Science.[41] During her final negotiations regarding the deanship at the University of Pittsburgh, she was contacted about Josey's recruitment as a potential faculty member for SLIS and the provost wanted to know from her what she thought. Her response was, "Do everything you can to get him; it would be wonderful to have him on the faculty!"[42] They both started in the fall of 1986.[43] Josey's affiliation with the University of Pittsburgh began six years earlier when he served as an external committee member for Marva De-

Loach's doctoral dissertation committee. Her research examined the impact of Title II-B on minority recruitment into librarianship during the years of 1970–1977. DeLoach was one of Josey's students at Savannah State College whom he encouraged to pursue library science. Their mentor–mentee relationship spanned more than forty years and they went on to publish several articles and books on various aspects of librarianship together, including the second edition of the *Handbook of Black Librarianship.*[44] One student lauded Josey as an inspirational teacher. "In his role as a teacher he inspires; he transmits his convictions and sense of commitment to new generations. It is not inconceivable that one day a Librarian of Congress may acknowledge a debt to E. J.'s faith and vision."[45]

SCHOLARSHIP

As a prolific writer, Josey published more than four hundred articles and authored/edited thirteen books in the disciplines of history, education, and library science. His commitment to civil and human rights and the upward mobility of blacks and other librarians of color in the profession is evident in many of his writings. Josey covers a broad range of topics on issues that primarily focus on racial equality in America. Few individuals have contributed as much to the library literature on the issue of race and civil rights as Josey. There are several significant works that are noteworthy as they lend insight into his intellectual development. Josey reviewed his commitment to civil rights and the battle against racism and segregation in the field of librarianship in a chapter entitled, "The Civil Rights Movement and American Librarianship: The Opening Round" in *Activism in American Librarianship, 1962–1973.*[46] In it, he chronicled his thoughts and experiences leading up to the historic resolution that prevented the Southern state library associations from affiliating with ALA members.

Six years following this successful declaration in 1964, Josey believed there was still a lot to be done along the lines of civil rights in the profession. He encouraged other black librarians to write about their experiences as librarians in order to create a history of black librarianship as well as to develop communication between blacks and the rest of society. The basic questions he asked them to think about in writing their stories included:

1. Who is the black librarian?
2. Why did you choose librarianship as a career?
3. What opportunities gave you the chance to develop your full potential?
4. What drawbacks did you encounter?
5. What are your accomplishments?

6. What do you as a black librarian think of the future?[47]

This compilation of essays written by Josey and twenty-four of his colleagues was published as his landmark book *The Black Librarian in America*.[48] This publication is considered Josey's seminal work and officially began the modern period of African American librarianship. According to Josey, prior to its publication, "Black librarians were unseen, unheard, and unknown."[49] The book addressed the widespread existence of racism in the profession and incorporated stories of segregation, bias, discrimination, and ignorance about black librarianship. "Writing the first book about black librarians remains one of the most rewarding accomplishments of my career."[50]

The Black Librarian in America Revisited,[51] a collection of thirty autobiographical and topical essays, presented important African American figures from the original collection and added the experiences of new African American librarians. In "A Mouthful of Civil Rights and an Empty Stomach,"[52] he accused libraries of "tokenism" because of the way libraries were dealing with the civil rights movement.[53] In a survey to see how many public libraries opened professional positions to black librarians, it was found that 10.6 percent employed black professionals in central libraries and 25.3 percent employed them in branches that served white patrons.[54] Josey said, "I firmly believe that there is no *real* integration of public libraries without an attempt to integrate the staff at all levels of employment."[55] As a result, Josey demanded immediate action to eliminate discrimination against African American librarians in Southern public libraries. Having spent a significant part of his career working in black college libraries, Josey frequently wrote about concerns related to black students and their challenges using the library. "The Future of the Black College Library"[56] emphasized the important role of libraries and librarians on black college campuses. He suggested that the college library has a role to play in educating black students:

[T]he black college library, an inextricable part of the black college, must dedicate its program to militate against this kind of hopelessness, bewilderment, and futility and free the minds of young American black men and women. . . . Historically, libraries in black colleges have not been supported with good budgets, excellent facilities and strong staffs, primarily because legislatures, foundations, and society have failed to support the black colleges per se. . . . The three main components of a library—resources, facilities, and staff—were woefully inadequate and remain inadequate in many black colleges today. . . . The most crucial test that the library must meet in responding to the needs of its disadvantaged who, because of their poor high school education, need extra help and assistance. One vital aspect of special assistance to young black students is the inauguration of special library counseling programs which could include unique orientation utilizing programmed instruction. . . . An excellent library is central to the intellectual life of a black college, and the future of the black college may very well depend upon the quality of its library.[57]

During the 1970s, Josey wrote about ways to help librarians. *What Black Librarians Are Saying*[58] framed the issues of the day and provided a forum for African American librarians to express their views and observations about the challenges they faced in the profession. Essays included in this work are divided into seven sections addressing a variety of topics including how to design materials to be of the greatest possible use to the black community, as well as urging librarians to adopt a variety of approaches when trying to communicate and effectively serve children from poor communities. Other parts of this compilation contain essays that examine professional organization issues and appeals to librarians to organize unions in the workplace. Using the BCALA as a model, ideas are presented on the necessity for professionals to form caucuses within their respective associations and within the library system.[59]

Handbook of Black Librarianship provides insight into some of the critical issues confronted by African Americans librarians. The first edition was compiled and edited by Josey and Ann Allen Shockley.[60] According to Josey, *Handbook of Black Librarianship* is his most prized work. "It is something every librarian should have in his or her personal collection."[61]

In its second edition,[62] this handbook was designed to provide information on the relationship of African Americans to various aspects of librarianship. It defines and documents black contributions to library and library education, past and present.

In the aftermath of the civil rights movement, Josey was compelled to write about issues of equity in the workplace. The issue of recruitment and retention of people of color in the profession was at the center of his writings. The driving force behind Josey's fight for equity was the executive order issued by President Kennedy in 1961 that established the Commission on Equal Employment Opportunity. The order basically stated that affirmative action should be used to ensure that applicants are employed, and that employees are fairly treated during employment, without regard to their race, creed, color, or national origin.

Josey stressed the critical need for library employers to support affirmative action for the recruitment of minorities to the profession. Substantial evidence of the underrepresentation of minorities in the library profession can be found in a number of studies reported and commented on by Josey. His most notable work is in a chapter he coauthored with DeLoach entitled, "Discrimination and Affirmative Action: Concerns for Black Librarians and Library Workers."[63] He advocated the necessity for affirmative action programs and reported commentaries of twenty-three leading librarians who were employed in public and university library systems.[64] These librarians described frustration with being overlooked for promotions and director positions. Josey campaigned for full faculty status for librarians who did the work of faculty: teaching, research, and publishing. From a survey of librarians, he found that many thought the question of review, election of a chief librarian, and so forth should be left to the administration of the college or university. He said, "Personally, I am not one to count on or trust a given administration to act in the best interest of the library or the library faculty; the reform of our colleges and universities insofar as libraries are concerned is in the hands of librarians."[65]

Josey wrote about faculty status and the need for standards similar to those used in determining faculty compensation, tenure, and education requirements. He asserted, "The academic librarian needs to seek new intellectual grounds to explore and build a real live learning environmental experience."[66]

Josey published many articles with his students and the librarians he recruited and mentored, and he established strong relationships with editors over the years. Longtime friend and mentor, Eric Moon, editor of *Library Journal* from 1959 to 1968, published many of his writings during the movement towards civil rights in the ALA. Josey served as editor of *The Bookmark* from 1976 to 1986. However, when he accepted the offer to join the University of Pittsburgh, he resigned the editorship. He also served as contributing editor to "Afro-Americans in New York Life and History" and served on the educational advisory committee of the *Multicultural Review*. He leveraged his position as scholar to advance his philosophy on civil rights and issues of equity for African American librarians and other marginalized groups.

SERVICE

Josey provided unyielding service to universities, departments, and the profession. Long before Josey became professor at the University of Pittsburgh, he was outspoken about librarianship as a profession and often encouraged African Americans to consider library science. In his first professional position at the Free Library of Philadelphia, he promoted librarianship. Friend, Jim McCoy, who first met Josey in 1954 at the Free Library of Philadelphia, says, "I was trying to decide on a graduate school, preferably in the social sciences. [Josey] urged me to consider the library profession because of new opportunities it presented for Blacks. It was a suggestion I have never regretted."[67]

An important aspect of Josey's position at the University of Pittsburgh was to recruit African American students to the school. His tenacious recruitment efforts allowed SLIS to be one of the leaders among universities' grad-uate and professional schools in minority recruitment efforts during the 1990s. Josey steadily led the drive to recruit and secure funding for several students of color. As minority recruitment officer, he was successful in ob-taining grants from the Commonwealth Fund[68] that allowed him to make site visits to countless universities and libraries throughout the nation to find promising students interested in pursuing library science as a career.[69]

Some of the sites that he visited were Lincoln University, the Enoch Pratt Free Library, and the Free Library of Philadelphia.[70] Josey was successful in each of his recruiting trips.[71] An idea to produce a recruitment brochure was inspired from his visit to the Petersburg Public Library, where he met a young library director, Wayne Cocker. Profiled in the Office of the Library Personnel Resources recruitment brochure, Cocker gave Josey the idea to produce a similar pamphlet for SLIS.[72] He later told Dean Bearman that he used this as a catalyst to explicate "the possibilities of librarians playing a major role in empowering the black community and communities with infor-mation, education and programs that would make a meaningful difference in the lives of people."[73]

Another recruitment effort that Josey spearheaded was to secure funding from the Commonwealth Fund and the University's Provost's Development Fund to support a proposal for the recruitment of black children's librarians and recruitment materials for black librarians in general. The project was to develop a special program to take a two-pronged approach to recruit and retain African American students for librarianship and to work with children. The initial focus of the proposal was to recruit African American students specifically to specialize in literature services for children and youth. The second phase of the proposal dealt with the development of general recruit-ment program materials. The result was produced in a video for black recruit-ment to the library profession narrated by famed actor, Ossie Davis, and distributed nationwide.[74]

Josey challenged cultural diversity in the recruitment of faculty and stu-dents from diverse backgrounds. He often relied on census data about the increase in minorities in the United States and requested that library schools recruit students and faculty to reflect the future faces of the country. He maintained that having minority faculty is the key to recruiting minority students to library schools and having minority librarians is the key to giving minorities access to information. Josey's love for students and his strong commitment to librarianship was the driving force behind his recruitment efforts at Pittsburgh. He adamantly believed that LIS programs should reaf-firm their commitment to increasing underrepresented groups' access to the LIS profession by utilizing an inclusive program for their recruitment.[75] He suggested that library schools should apply a three-step program to become more involved with recruitment:

1. Establish formal mechanisms with the large public libraries and research academic libraries to seek the development of a liaison program for the recruitment of minorities.
2. Urge larger urban public libraries and major research libraries to establish a tuition support program for minority staff who attends LIS programs with a promise that persons will return to libraries to work for a minimum of two years after graduation.
3. Send a representative to large urban public libraries and major research libraries to contact minorities by addressing staff associations and library unions and by participating in continuing education programs.[76]

During Josey's professorship at the University of Pittsburgh, he increased the minority enrollment significantly at SLIS. According to Joyce C. Wright, a colleague and fellow recruiter for the University of Illinois at Urbana-Champaign, "When Professor Josey joined the faculty at the University of Pittsburgh School of Library and Information Science in the 1980s, there were three minority students. [About five years after he arrived,] there [we]re twenty-seven minority students enrolled in the School of Library and Information Science—five Asians, five Hispanics and seventeen African Americans."[77] Josey continued his recruiting efforts long after he retired from the University of Pittsburgh, and many of his ideas are still very much a part of the school. Although the numbers are not nearly as high as they were when he was active, the university still matriculates a high number of blacks, Latinos, and Asians. After his retirement, SLIS established an endowed scholarship in Josey's honor.

Since the post–civil rights era, there have been countless efforts to increase the racial and ethnic diversity in the LIS profession. Despite numerous initiatives on this front, recruitment and retention of librarians of color is challenging for library directors. As a profession, librarianship has not attracted a large number of individuals from various ethnic and racial groups largely because there have not been sustainable efforts to recruit them. Given this, Josey's recruitment accomplishments at Pittsburgh seem even more remarkable. The fact that there remains significant underrepresentation among ethnic and racial groups strongly suggests that there might be structural aspects of the educational system that tend to discourage minorities from being recruited. For example, it may be that schools and departments of LIS are not devoting enough time and resources to recruitment. Effective recruitment strategies like those that Josey designed in the eighties and nineties can be emulated and may increase the number of candidates from marginalized groups today.

DIVERSITY AND INCLUSION IN LIS EDUCATION

The epistemological foundation of the concept of diversity is based on the assumption that what we perceive as "diversity" or "diverse" is not objective. *Diversity*, as it is has come to be used in public and scholarly discourse since the 1970s, refers specifically to those differences, primarily in race and ethnicity, that have been the basis of exclusion or segregation or differential treatment in public action and private social interaction.[78] Its use and importance are closely linked to the divisions of race that have significantly shaped American history, society, and culture.[79] "This specific current meaning of *diversity* grows out of the great effort in the 1950s and 1960s to overcome the inferior position, in law and social treatment, of American Blacks."[80]

Although diversity had a different meaning in the nineteenth century, it has been a perennial concern for LIS since the founding of the profession. Diversity has become more inclusive with not only race and ethnicity, but also gender, sexual orientation, age, mental, and physical abilities, and so forth. Early challenges of diversity can be seen primarily in the recruitment of women to the field of library science. The School of Library Economy created by Dewey recruited women in the library science program.[81] While there is speculation as to why he recruited women into the Columbia College program, there is evidence that Dewey had personal and financial reasons for bringing women into the program. Michael H. Harris affirms Dewey's questionable motives when he writes this:

> His almost mystical influence over his followers, the unremitting hatred evidenced toward him by his enemies, the charges against him of anti-Semitism, his strange and controversial involvement with (and influence over) women, and his ruthless and often questionable entrepreneurial schemes, all contribute to his reputation as one of the most complex figures in the history of librarianship.[82]

The demographic shift in the United States since the nineteenth century not only affected the larger society, but it also had a significant impact on professional organizations. The Association for Library and Information Science Education was not exempt. The first African American library science faculty member was Edward Christopher Williams at the Western Reserve University (later renamed Case Western Reserve University) in 1904.[83] Nearly forty years later, Eliza Atkins Gleason was the first black woman to receive a doctorate in 1940. She went on to establish and become the first dean of the School of Library Service at Atlanta University. She created a library science curriculum that trained more than 90 percent of all black librarians by 1986.[84] Claudia Gollop contends that "even though the number of blacks to hold faculty positions has increased since 1904, it is far from being representative of the African American population in the United States."[85] The twenty-first century—where we see the once minority steadily become the majority—offers a heightened awareness of the importance of global and national understanding of cross-cultural perspectives. Such trends and transitions contribute to the shaping of American higher education.

The racial and ethnic diversity of faculty is driven by the increasing diversity of the student body. In fact, Paul T. Jaeger and Renee E. Franklin[86] examined how a lack of faculty of color in library and information science programs results in a lack of students of color in library science. In other words, without diverse faculty, there's little hope of increasing diversity within the field. This is a systemic problem that has consequences beyond individual people where there needs to be further exploration into the role race and racism play in our pedagogical interactions. The diversity of college and university faculty has been the focus of discussion and debate for several decades, particularly since the 1960s when equity in higher education became a national priority as a result of the civil rights movement. Scholars such as Lorna Peterson,[87] Jaeger, Franklin, and John Carlo Bertot[88] and a host of others have attempted to define diversity in order to help professionals understand the changing racial, ethnic and cultural milieu in LIS. "Populations affected by issues of diversity and representation in LIS now include disability, age, gender, socioeconomic status, language, literacy, sexual orientation, and geography, along with the areas of race, ethnicity and multiculturalism that have received most of the traditional focus in LIS."[89] Conversations around diversity should be less concerned with defining diversity and more focused on acknowledging that we live in a diverse society where there is racial, ethnic, gender, cultural, age, physical, and mental diversity. It is simply the differences among us.[90]

Despite exhaustive discourse and numerous programs to advance faculty diversity, the national outlook remains dismal. The overwhelming majority of full-time faculty in the United States identify as white, and approximately 20 percent are black, Asian/Pacific Islander, Hispanic, American Indian/ Alaska Native, and multiracial.[91] Black faculty make up 4 percent of faculty membership. The gender disparity is far more equal with 50 percent male and 50 percent female.[92] However, the LIS profession as a whole is overwhelmingly female. According to the ALA 2017 demographic study, 81 percent of its members are female and 19 percent are male.[93] In 2014, the study yielded the same results.[94]

Unfortunately, black women faculty are far scarcer. This trend among LIS faculty of color mirrors what exists in other disciplines and stems from a long history of systemic exclusion. Statistics for ALISE have revealed that there has not been much change in the recruitment and retention of faculty of color. This was a grave concern for Josey. In 1993, he asserted,

> If you carefully examine the ALISE annual statistics, you will find that blacks,
> Hispanics, Asians, and American Indians have not increased as a percentage of
> the entire population in library and information science education programs
> since the passage of the Civil Rights Act of 1964.[95]

Merely having conversations around diversity and inclusion was never going to be enough for Josey. As someone who had lived the majority of his life fighting injustice, it was no surprise that when he joined the faculty at the University of Pittsburgh and became involved in ALISE that he would bring the same energy he had at ALA. Although it was twenty years after he introduced the historic resolution disbanding segregation in the ALA, many of the same issues around race and inclusion persisted. In fact, some argued that things were worse. Perhaps the greatest challenge for faculty of color was in acquiring tenure. Ione Damasco and Dracine Hodges contend that the rigorous processes of tenure for minority faculty "are further complicated by implicit barriers and issues that racial and ethnic minorities often face when working in predominantly White environments."[96]

The genesis for tenure in the United States was developed by the American Association of University Professors (AAUP) as part of the "1940 Statement of Principles on Academic Freedom and Tenure" (1940 Statement).[97] Tenure seeks to guarantee that educators will be afforded academic freedom in their teaching and research pursuits—important components in realizing the common good that education provides. Furthermore, it is a condition of employment that provides enough economic security to make fulfillment of a faculty member's obligation to students and society a more attractive proposition—the faculty member is expected to continue to give something on an ongoing basis in return for receiving tenure.[98]

Tenure is not simply a guarantee of lifetime employment, as commonly perceived. Appointment to tenure is an unlimited academic employment that can be terminated only for extraordinary conditions such as financial necessity or the discontinuation of a program. The 1940 Statement was supported by the Association of American Colleges and Universities and more than 250

Table 5.1. Ethnicity of Full-Time LIS Faculty. *ALISE Statistical Report 2017*

Asian	13%
Black or African American	4%
Hispanic	3%
Native American	0%
International	1%
Unknown	10%
White	63%

scholarly and higher education organizations and is widely adopted into faculty handbooks and collective bargaining agreements at institutions of higher education throughout the United States.[99] The 1940 Statement asserted that tenure would defend academic freedom on three primary pillars:

1. Faculty members are entitled to complete freedom in research and to publish their findings subject to the satisfactory performance of their other academic responsibilities.
2. Faculty members are entitled to intellectual freedom in the classroom in discussing topics, but they should be careful not to introduce into their teaching controversial issues which have no relation to their subject.
3. As members of the college or university, faculty are members of a learned profession, and officers of an educational institution. As such, they should be free from institutional censorship or discipline.

The AAUP believed that these assertions would allow scholars the freedom to hold diverse perspectives while benefitting society. While many view attaining tenure as a great achievement, the status of tenure has been debated. For example, several have maintained that the job security provided by tenure is necessary to recruit talented faculty because in many fields nonacademic jobs pay significantly more.[100] In contrast, others like economist Steven D. Levitt have argued that modern tenure systems diminish academic freedom and "distorts people's effort so that they face strong incentives early in their career (and presumably work very hard early on as a consequence) and very weak incentives forever after (and presumably work much less hard on an average as a consequence)."[101]

MULTICULTURAL, ETHNIC, AND HUMANISTIC CONCERNS (MEHC) AND SPECIAL INTEREST GROUP (SIG)

While at Delaware State College and at Savannah State College, Josey advocated for faculty status for academic librarians. So, when he came to academia as a full-time faculty member, it was no surprise that he was a staunch supporter of professors attaining tenure. It was especially important for faculty of color who experienced inequality on university campuses and suffered racial battle fatigue.[102] Josey believed that these were serious concerns of LIS educators. So, he did not hesitate to accept the invitation by the president of ALISE, Miles M. Jackson, who in 1989 asked Josey to lead a committee to explore the state of affairs in ethnic, multicultural, and humanistic concerns in LIS.[103] The committee was charged with preparing a special report:

1. The extent of inclusion of ethnic and multicultural concerns in the library and information science curricula in ALISE schools.
2. Respond to these questions: What is being done to recruit minorities to the profession? What library association committees exist for recruiting racial minorities?
3. Explore the possibility of establishing a special interest group (SIG) for ethnic and multicultural concerns in Library and Information Science education.[104]

"A preliminary report from the committee was made at the Board of Directors meeting at the ALISE annual conference in January 1990 in Chicago."[105] The following year, the Multicultural, Ethnic, and Humanistic Concerns (MEHC) SIG was established at the 1991 ALISE annual conference.[106] In 2011, the SIG celebrated its twentieth anniversary. It brought together many of the original members, current SIG co-conveners, then president, Lorna Peterson, and a host of conferees. Peterson's directive was to embrace the 2011 ALISE conference theme of competitiveness and innovation in celebrating the twentieth anniversary of the MEHC SIG and the need to continue the work started in 1989. Clara Chu worked with Ismail Abdullahi, Renate Chancellor, and Shari Lee to develop a two-part program.[107] Part one was the ALISE president's program where leaders addressed the issue of "diversity as a condition for the success and strength of ALISE, and LIS education and research."[108] "The second part of the program was a celebration of 20 years of the establishment of the MEHC SIG, with initial discussion on the need for an ALISE Statement on Diversity."[109] The statement "would call for ALISE to incorporate diversity into its mission and consider it a core value by its individual and institutional members."[110] "Furthermore, the value of and commitment to diversity should be expressed in practice, including the climate of LIS programs, the make-up of faculty and students, and in the teaching, service and research priorities."[111] "Each approach for developing a diversity statement had distinctive characteristics:"[112]

Model #1: Stand-alone statement of diversity principles that incorporates equity and inclusiveness. This approach provides principles that inform/regulate all actions of ALISE and its membership.
Model #2: A benefits approach (why). This approach is outcomes based, which emphasizes the benefits, thus, providing rationale for a commitment to diversity.
Model #3: A competencies approach (how). This approach is action-based, which emphasizes the knowledge and behavior required in an environment committed to diversity and equity.
Model #4: An integrative approach—diversity as an equity and ethical issue. This approach engages existing ALISE policy by proposing to

integrate diversity and inclusion more explicitly into the ALISE Ethics Guidelines Statement (Fall 2010) and amend sit as the ALISE Statement of Ethics and Diversity.[113]

In many ways the MEHC twentieth-anniversary celebration renewed the association's commitment to diversity that was initiated by Josey. Following the success of the celebration, the ALISE Board established a diversity task force. With the feedback from ALISE 2011 presidential program, the task force decided to develop a diversity statement that would address principles, benefits, and competencies. It was at the 2012 ALISE conference where the MEHC SIG and the deans and directors SIG sponsored a session to gather feedback from a draft of the diversity statement. The feedback resulted in a revised draft that was presented and approved by the ALISE Board in September 2012.[114] The diversity statement was unanimously approved at the ALISE conference in 2013. To introduce the statement and provide models on how to move the statement from words to action—in the classroom, scholarship, and institution—a session was held at the conference entitled "What of Diversity? (Always the Beautiful, and Essential, Question): An Ignite Session on Ideas You Can Use to Advance Diversity Mentorship."

The *Oxford English Dictionary* defines "mentor" as "a person who acts as guide and advisor to another person, esp[ecially] one who is younger and less experienced."[115] Mentorship for MLIS students, doctoral students, and faculty is well documented in LIS literature.[116] Josey encompasses many of these qualities. He mentored countless librarians and students of library science throughout his professional career. As mentor, he helped students become effective practitioners as well as assisted with their development as professionals in the field. Traditionally, mentoring has been defined as a relationship between a senior, more experienced advisor and a younger, less experienced protégé for the purpose of helping and developing his or her career. Often the mentor may be employed in the same organization as the protégé or be in the chain of command or profession. Although the definition of mentoring has been refined over the years, a core feature that defines mentoring relationships and distinguishes it from other types of personal relationships is that mentoring is a developmental relationship that is embedded within the career context.

Edith Maureen Fisher was a new librarian when she first met Josey at the BCALA meeting while a library student at the University of Illinois in Urbana-Champaign in 1972.[117] Fisher remembered that after the meeting he took time to educate her about the importance of the BCALA and her role as a librarian.[118] After being hired for an academic library position later that year, she contacted Josey about her new position, and he advised her again. She recalled his words of wisdom:

When I contacted E. J. about my new position he educated me again, this time not only about what hurdles could be expected when one is integrating a library for the first time and the importance of giving your all to those you serve, but also about the newly formed group of California black librarians, about the broader context of national issues being important at the state level, and about the importance of networking. He helped educate me not only about my crucial role in the library but about the importance of broadening my professional horizons and contributions.[119]

Fisher attributes Josey's support and interest as instrumental in fostering her career in librarianship. She went on to have a very accomplished career as a librarian, which included chairing several committees in ALA and ACRL, as well as serving as president of the BCALA.[120] Josey also helped guide many of the students who used the libraries at Delaware State College and Savannah State College. Similarly, Malikah Dada Lumumba was inspired by Josey as a young library page. She recalls how she was "impressed with Dr. Josey's eloquent presentation, immaculate attire, and cool, dignified stature that I wanted to be like him. I knew that I wanted to be a librarian now, more than ever."[121]

Josey encouraged Patricia Quarterman to pursue librarianship as a career and she credits him with being instrumental in choosing her career path. She explains:

I gained a deeper appreciation of the library and librarians as a result of watching the growth and development of the library's activities. . . . It was because of my admiration for Mr. Josey and my love for books and book-related service that I elected librarianship as a career in my junior year. When I told Mr. Josey of my decision, he was elated. He encouraged me to go to library school and study for the master's degree in library science. He assisted me in selecting a library school and acted as my sponsor and mentor.[122]

According to the Metro-Paterson Academy for Communications and Technology MPACT Report, Josey served on a total of thirty-five doctoral committees, eight of which he chaired, and the remainder he served as a faculty advisor while at the University of Pittsburgh.[123] Many of his students have gone on to take strong leadership roles as deans, professors, librarians, and directors of libraries and other information institutions. For instance, Mark Winston, who received his PhD from the University of Pittsburgh in 1997, was not only mentored by Josey but worked as his teaching assistant while in the master's program. He was profoundly influenced by Josey in two ways. Winston says that "in coming into the discipline, Josey felt that librarians should be researchers, and publish and in turn, he motivated me to do that."[124] Another way Winston was affected by Josey was that "librarians had the ability to have a real societal impact."[125] Winston further says that Josey believed that "librarians were not only uniquely positioned to transform society, but they had an obligation to."[126]

Josey's first doctoral student, Ismail Abdullahi, came to know Josey in 1982 at the IFLA Conference in Ontario, Canada. As fellow members of IFLA, they served together on a number of committees, and in 1985 Josey invited him to the United States to study library science. Josey subsequently recruited him to the doctoral program at the University of Pittsburgh. It is also important to note that Josey did not only mentor people of color. Many of these sentiments were echoed by librarians who were socially progressive and wanted change in the ALA. Patricia Glass Schuman was a member of the New York Roundtable on Social Responsibilities, of which Josey was one of the founders. According to Schuman, Josey sought out promising librarians to take on leading roles in the ALA. She recalls that he was "a colleague, a mentor, and an enduring example of commitment."[127] Schuman went on to become president of ALA largely due to the support and encouragement of Josey. She remembers how Josey was fearless and not afraid to speak his mind, encouraging others to do the same. For example:

> E. J. arranged for me to give my first speech by suggesting me as a substitute for himself as a speaker on faculty status for librarians at the New England Library Association. At that time faculty status was a very controversial issue. I was very nervous and almost refused. E. J. told me I could do it—so I did. Despite my limited experience in ALA, E. J. nominated me to run for ALA Council and helped me get elected.[128]

Because of Josey's commitment to the profession and his unselfish nature in helping young librarians become active in the profession, he was able to develop a following of librarians unlike few others in the profession. According to Schuman, "E. J. has helped to create within the profession a nucleus of people whom he has encouraged and nurtured: librarians who believe that we can be an essential part of the solution to critical problems, librarians willing to work for change."[129] Colleague and former president of the ALA, Barbara Ford, when asked about Josey's greatest contribution to the profession, observed,

> I would say serving as a role model and mentor for so many librarians through the years. Librarians from all kinds of backgrounds with all kinds of interests; he was always willing to talk with you to give you his best advice and opinion and you know all people who reach the levels that he did; ALA Presidency and the position he had in the NY State and at the University of Pittsburgh; not everyone is that open. But E. J. really took that mentoring, recruitment role very, very seriously and I think that probably has the most impact.[130]

Through his publishing, Josey mentored and served as a role model for countless librarians. His dynamic teaching style combined with his creative curriculum increased his presence as a scholar. There is consensus among Josey's mentees that he has undoubtedly made a difference in their lives. Although he retired in 1995 from teaching, Josey remained active in recruiting and mentoring students up until his death.

Josey's success in recruiting and mentoring students led to the creation of several scholarships that were established in his honor. The BCALA created a self-regulating scholarship fund; *The E. J. Josey Scholarship* is given annually to an African American or Canadian citizen pursuing a degree in an ALA accredited LIS program in the United States or Canada. Upon his retirement from the University of Pittsburgh's School of Library and Information Science in 1995, he was named professor emeritus, and the E. J. Josey Endowment Scholarship for Minorities was named on his behalf. The scholarship is awarded annually to an enrolled black graduate student in the Department of LIS who demonstrates potential for academic excellence and leadership in the profession. The ACRL established the Dr. E. J. Josey Mentoring Program for Spectrum Scholars. The scholarship provides an opportunity to assist with the development of the next generation of academic librarians. "The goal of this program is to link participating library school students and newly graduated librarians who are of American Indian/Alaska Native, Asian, Black/African American, Hispanic/Latino, Middle Eastern and North African, and/or Native Hawaiian/Other Pacific Islander descent, with established academic librarians who will provide mentoring and coaching support, serve as a role model in academic librarianship, and provide guidance in seeking a career path and opportunities for leadership in the profession. This program pairs recipients of ALA's Spectrum Scholarship Program with mentors from ACRL."[131]

A multiday E. J. Josey Doctoral Leadership Institute for twelve Spectrum Doctoral Fellows was held as a pre-ALISE conference on January 20, 2009, in Denver, Colorado. The goal of the institute was to connect advanced doctoral students and junior faculty. The institute was designed to address leadership and doctoral studies as well as enable engagement among the fellows through dialogue, reflection, and opportunities for networking. The goal of the institute was twofold: first, to provide direction for the future of diversity and doctoral education and research; and second, discuss the development of a predoctoral institute to address diversity in LIS recruitment, scholarship, and faculty representation.

Josey exhibited *individual consideration*, where the leader is a role model, mentor, or teacher to bring the follower into the group throughout much of his professional career. As an educator, he demonstrated this tenet through his active recruitment of students to LIS as well as his mentorship of librarians and LIS educators. Not only did he educate them about LIS, but he motivated many of them to become transformative leaders. They became his friends, colleagues, co-authors, and supporters of the same issues he advocated.

NOTES

1. Association for Library and Information Science Education, "ALISE Leadership Academy," accessed June 30, 2019, https://ali.memberclicks.net/index.php?option=com_jevents&task=icalevent.detail&evid=15.

2. Christina Neigel, "LIS Leadership and Leadership Education: A Matter of Gender," *Journal of Library Administration* 55, no. 7 (October 2015): 521, https://doi.org/10.1080/01930826.2015.1076307 (emphasis omitted). The original is italicized and found in the abstract on page 521.

3. Deborah Hicks and Lisa M. Given, "Principled, Transformational Leadership: Analyzing the Discourse of Leadership in the Development of Librarianship's Core Competences," *Library Quarterly: Information, Community, Policy* 83, no. 1 (January 2013): 8, 11–12, doi: 10.1086/668678.

4. Hicks and Given, "Principled, Transformational Leadership," 18–19.

5. Hicks and Given, "Principled, Transformational Leadership," 9, 16.

6. Richard E. Rubin, *Foundations of Library and Information Science*, 4th ed. (Chicago: Neal-Schuman, 2016), 49–50.

7. Rubin, *Foundations of Library and Information Science*, 242–45.

8. John V. Richardson, "History of American Library Science: Its Origins and Early Development," *Encyclopedia of Library and Information Sciences*, 3rd ed. (2010): 6, doi:10.1081/E-ELIS3-120043738; Rubin, *Foundations of Library and Information Science*, 245.

9. Rubin, *Foundations of Library and Information Science*, 245–46.

10. Rubin, *Foundations of Library and Information Science*, 246–47.

11. Richardson, "History of American Library Science," 6; Rubin, *Foundations of Library and Information Science*, 247.

12. Richardson, "History of American Library Science," 8; Rubin, *Foundations of Library and Information Science*, 247.

13. Richardson, "History of American Library Science," 7; Rubin, *Foundations of Library and Information Science*, 247–50.

14. Richardson, "History of American Library Science," 7; Rubin, *Foundations of Library and Information Science*, 250.

15. William R. and Norma B. Harvey Library, "Research Guides: The Hampton University Forum on Minority Recruitment and Retention in the LIS Field: University History in Training of Minority Librarians," last updated October 1, 2018, https://hamptonu.libguides.com/c.php?g=815577&p=5832646.

16. Robert Sidney Martin and Orvin Lee Shiflett, "Hampton, Fisk, and Atlanta: The Foundations, the American Library Association, and Library Education for Blacks, 1925–1941," *Libraries and Culture* 31, no. 2 (Spring 1996): 299–322, https://www.jstor.org/stable/25548438.

17. William R. and Norma B. Harvey Library, "Research Guides."

18. Benjamin F. Speller, "E. J. Josey: A True Friend of North Carolina Central University," in *E. J. Josey: An Activist Librarian*, ed. Ismail Abdullahi (Metuchen, NJ: Scarecrow, Press, 1992), 139.

19. Speller, "E. J. Josey," 141–46.

20. Speller, "E. J. Josey," 146–47.

21. Alma Dawson, "Celebrating African-American Librarians and Librarianship," *Library Trends* 49, no. 1 (Summer 2000): 49–50, http://proxycu.wrlc.org/login?url=https://search-proquest-com.proxycu.wrlc.org/docview/220461892?accountid=9940.

22. William R. and Norma B. Harvey Library, "Research Guides."

23. William R. and Norma B. Harvey Library, "Research Guides."

24. Rubin, *Foundations of Library and Information Science*, 251.

25. William R. and Norma B. Harvey Library, "Research Guides."

26. Rubin, *Foundations of Library and Information Science*, 251–52.

27. Rubin, *Foundations of Library and Information Science*, 252.

28. Marion Paris, "Why Library Schools Fail," *Library Journal* 115, no. 16 (October 1990): 38–42.

29. Rubin, *Foundations of Library and Information Science*, 252.

30. Michael K. Buckland, "Information as Thing," *Journal of the American Society for Information Science* 42, no. 5 (June 1991): 351–60, doi:10.1002/(SICI)1097-4571.

31. History of iSchools, https://ischools.org/resources/Documents/History-of-the-iSchools-2009.pdf.

32. https://ischools.org/About.

33. Richardson, "History of American Library Science," 8.

34. iSchools Goals, https://ischools.org/About.

35. Clara Stanton Jones, "E. J. Josey: Librarian for All Seasons," in *E. J. Josey: An Activist Librarian*, ed. Ismail Abdullahi (Metuchen, NJ: Scarecrow Press, 1992), 3–4.

36. Memorandum by Allen Kent to the faculty and staff at the University of Pittsburgh School of Library and Information Science, 1986.

37. Joyce Wright, in discussion with the author, April 11, 2007.

38. E. J. Josey, in personal communication with the author, April 2001.

39. Barry L. Chad, "E. J. Josey, the Professor," in *E. J. Josey: An Activist Librarian*, ed. Ismail Abdullahi (Metuchen, NJ: Scarecrow Press, 1992), 125.

40. Toni Carbo Bearman, "E. J. Josey as a Faculty Colleague," in *E. J. Josey: An Activist Librarian*, ed. Ismail Abdullahi (Metuchen, NJ: Scarecrow Press, 1992), 150.

41. Bearman, "E. J. Josey as a Faculty Colleague," 149.

42. Bearman, "E. J. Josey as a Faculty Colleague," 150.

43. Bearman, "E. J. Josey as a Faculty Colleague," 150.

44. E. J. Josey and Marva L. DeLoach, eds., *Handbook of Black Librarianship*, 2nd ed. (Lanham, MD: Scarecrow Press, 2000).

45. Chad, "E. J. Josey, the Professor," 129.

46. E. J. Josey, "The Civil Rights Movement and American Librarianship: The Opening Round," in *Activism in American Librarianship, 1962–1973*, ed. Mary Lee Bundy and Frederick J. Stielow (New York: Greenwood Press, 1987), 13–20.

47. E. J. Josey, ed., *The Black Librarian in America* (Metuchen, NJ: Scarecrow Press, 1970).

48. E. J. Josey, ed., *The Black Librarian in America*.

49. Josey, in personal communication with the author, April 2001.

50. Leonard Kniffel, "To Be Black and a Librarian: Talking with E. J. Josey," *American Libraries* 31, no. 1 (January 2000): 82, https://www.jstor.org/stable/25637460.

51. E. J. Josey, ed., *The Black Librarian in America Revisited* (Metuchen: NJ: Scarecrow Press, 1994).

52. E. J. Josey, "A Mouthful of Civil Rights and an Empty Stomach," *Library Journal* 90, no. 2 (January 1965): 202–5.

53. Josey, "Mouthful of Civil Rights and an Empty Stomach," 205.

54. Josey, "Mouthful of Civil Rights and an Empty Stomach," 202–3.

55. Josey, "Mouthful of Civil Rights and an Empty Stomach," 204–5.

56. E. J. Josey, "The Future of the Black College Library," *Library Journal* 94, no. 16 (September 1969): 3019–22.

57. Josey, "Future of the Black College Library," 3019, 3020, 3022.

58. E. J. Josey, ed., *What Black Librarians Are Saying* (Metuchen, NJ: Scarecrow Press, 1972).

59. Josey, *What Black Librarians Are Saying*. This citation is for the entire paragraph, which refers to different parts of the book.

60. E. J. Josey and Ann Allen Shockley, eds., *Handbook of Black Librarianship* (Littleton, CO: Libraries Unlimited, 1977).

61. E. J. Josey, personal interview with the author, March 10, 2001.

62. Josey and DeLoach, eds., *Handbook of Black Librarianship*, 2nd ed.

63. E. J. Josey and Marva L. DeLoach, "Discrimination and Affirmative Action: Concerns for Black Librarians and Library Workers," in *Librarians' Affirmative Action Handbook*, ed. John H. Harvey and Elizabeth M. Dickinson (Metuchen, NJ: Scarecrow Press, 1983), 179–99.

64. Josey and DeLoach, "Discrimination and Affirmative Action," 179–80.

65. Josey and DeLoach, "Discrimination and Affirmative Action," 179–80.

66. Josey and DeLoach, "Discrimination and Affirmative Action," 179–80.

67. Jim F. McCoy, "Remembrances and Reflections of an NAACP Leader," in *E. J. Josey: An Activist Librarian*, ed. Ismail Abdullahi, (Metuchen, NJ: Scarecrow Press, 1992), 121.

68. The Commonwealth Fund is a private, charitable foundation that aims to promote a high performing health care system that achieves better access, improved quality, and greater efficiency, particularly for marginalized populations. *See* https://www.commonwealthfund.org/.

69. Bearman, "E. J. Josey as a Faculty Colleague," 152.

70. Bearman, "E. J. Josey as a Faculty Colleague," 152.

71. Toni Carbo Bearman, personal interview with the author, April 6, 2007.

72. Bearman, "E. J. Josey as a Faculty Colleague," 152–53.

73. Bearman, "E. J. Josey as a Faculty Colleague," 153.

74. Bearman, "E. J. Josey as a Faculty Colleague," 153.

75. E. J. Josey, "Minority Representation in Library and Information Science Programs," *The Bookmark* 48, no. 1 (Fall 1989): 54–57.

76. Josey, "Minority Representation in Library and Information Science Programs."

77. Joyce C. Wright, "Recruiting Minorities to the Profession," in *E. J. Josey: An Activist Librarian*, ed. Ismail Abdullahi (Metuchen, NJ: Scarecrow Press, 1992), 168.

78. "Diversity: Before Diversity, from Affirmative Action to Diversity, the Diverse Society Governing a Diverse Society." https://science.jrank.org/pages/7633/Diversity.html.

79. "Diversity." https://science.jrank.org/pages/7633/Diversity.html.

80. "Diversity." https://science.jrank.org/pages/7633/Diversity.html.

81. Sarah K. Vann, ed., *Melvil Dewey: His Enduring Presence in Librarianship* (Littleton, CO: Libraries Unlimited, 1978), 39.

82. Michael H. Harris, ed., foreword to *Melvil Dewey: His Enduring Presence in Librarianship*, ed. Sarah K. Vann (Littleton, CO: Libraries Unlimited, 1978), 10.

83. Casper LeRoy Jordan and E. J. Josey, "A Chronology of Events in Black Librarianship," in *Handbook of Black Librarianship*, eds. E. J. Josey and Ann Allen Shockley (Littleton, CO: Libraries Unlimited, 1977), 16.

84. *World Encyclopedia of Library and Information Services* (Chicago: American Library Association, 1993), s.v. "Gleason, Eliza Atkins."

85. Claudia J. Gollop, "Library and Information Science Education: Preparing Librarians for a Multicultural Society," *College and Research Libraries* 60, no. 4 (July 1999): 388.

86. Paul T. Jaeger and Renee E. Franklin, "The Virtuous Circle: Increasing Diversity in LIS Faculties to Create More Inclusive Library Services and Outreach," *Education Libraries* 30, no. 1 (Summer 2007), 20–26.

87. Lorna Peterson, "The Definition of Diversity: Two Views—A More Specific Definition," *Journal of Library Administration* 27, nos. 1–2 (May 1999): 17–26, https://doi.org/10.1300/J111v27n01_03.

88. Paul T. Jaeger, John Carlo Bertot, and Renee E. Franklin, "Diversity, Inclusion, and Underrepresented Populations in LIS Research," *The Library Quarterly* 80, no. 2 (April 2010):175–81, doi:10.1086/651053.

89. Paul T. Jaeger, Mega M. Subramaniam, Cassandra B. Jones, and John Carlo Bertot, "Diversity and LIS Education: Inclusion and the Age of Information," *Journal of Education for Library and Information Science* 52, no. 2 (July 2011): 166, https://www.terpconnect.umd.edu/~mmsubram/Jaegeretal_JELIS.pdf.

90. Shari Lee and Renate Chancellor, "ALISE Diversity Statement," Association for Library and Information Science Education, approved September 30, 2012, adopted January 24, 2013, http://www.alise.org/alise---alise-diversity-statement.

91. National Center for Education Statistics, U.S. Department of Education, *The Condition of Education 2017* (May 2017), 255, https://nces.ed.gov/pubsearch/pubsinfo.asp?pubid=2017144.

92. Association for Library and Information Science Education, "2017 Statistical Reports," accessed January 15, 2019, https://www.alise.org/statistical-report-2

93. ALA Office of Research and Statistics Demographic Study Report 2017.

94. ALA Office of Research and Statistics Demographic Study Report 2017.

95. E. J. Josey, "The Challenges of Cultural Diversity in the Recruitment of Faculty and Students from Diverse Backgrounds," *Journal of Education for Library and Information Science* 34, no. 4 (Fall 1993): 303, https://www.jstor.org.proxycu.wrlc.org/stable/41308876.

96. American Association of University Professors, "1940 Statement of Principles on Academic Freedom and Tenure with 1970 Interpretive Comments," adopted April 1970, https://www.aaup.org/file/1940%20Statement.pdf.

97. American Association of University Professors, "1940 Statement."

98. American Association of University Professors, "1940 Statement."

99. American Association of University Professors, "1940 Statement."

100. American Association of University Professors, "1940 Statement."

101. Steven D. Levitt, "Let's Just Get Rid of Tenure (Including Mine), *Freakonomics*, March 3, 2007, http://freakonomics.com/2007/03/03/lets-just-get-rid-of-tenure/.

102. Renate L. Chancellor, "Racial Battle Fatigue: The Unspoken Burden of Black Women Faculty in LIS," *Journal of Education and Library and Information Science* 60, no. 3 (July 2019): 182–89.

103. Ismail Abdullahi, "Library Services to Multicultural Populations," in: *Encyclopedia of Library and Information Science*, vol. 48, Supplement 11, ed. Allen Kent (New York: Marcel Dekker, 1991), 267.

104. Abdullahi, "Library Services to Multicultural Populations," 267.

105. Abdullahi, "Library Services to Multicultural Populations," 267.

106. Association for Library and Information Science Education, "ALISE Diversity Statement Proposal," September 22, 2012, https://www.alise.org/assets/documents/alise-diversitystatement-proposal4members.pdf.

107. ALISE Diversity Statement Proposal," Association for Library and Information Science Education.

108. "ALISE Diversity Statement Proposal," Association for Library and Information Science Education.

109. "ALISE Diversity Statement Proposal," Association for Library and Information Science Education.

110. "ALISE Diversity Statement Proposal," Association for Library and Information Science Education.

111. "ALISE Diversity Statement Proposal," Association for Library and Information Science Education.

112. "ALISE Diversity Statement Proposal," Association for Library and Information Science Education.

113. "ALISE Diversity Statement Proposal," Association for Library and Information Science Education.

114. "ALISE Diversity Statement Proposal," Association for Library and Information Science Education.

115. *Oxford English Dictionary*, s.v. "mentor (*n.*)," accessed June 20, 2019, https://www.oed.com/view/Entry/116575?rskey=Zgz5Z2&result=1#eid.

116. Deborah Hicks, "The Practice of Mentoring: Reflecting on the Critical Aspects for Leadership Development," *The Australian Library Journal* 60, no. 1 (February 2011): 66–74; Meagan Lacy and Andrea J. Copeland, "The Role of Mentorship Programs in LIS Education and in Professional Development," *Journal of Education for Library and Information Science* 54, no. 2 (April 2013): 135–46; Judi Moreillon, "Educating for School Library Leadership: Developing the Instructional Partnership Role," *Journal of Education for Library and Information Science* 54, no. 1 (January 2013): 55–66, https://www.jstor.org.proxycu.wrlc.org/stable/43686932.

117. Edith Maureen Fisher, "E. J. Josey: Library Educator," in *E. J. Josey: An Activist Librarian*, ed. Ismail Abdullahi (Metuchen, NJ: Scarecrow Press, 1992), 130.

118. Fisher, "E. J. Josey," 131–32.

119. Fisher, "E. J. Josey," 132.

120. Fisher, "E. J. Josey," 132.

121. Malikah Dada Lumumba, "E. J. Josey: A Mentor and Friend," in *E. J. Josey: An Activist Librarian*, ed. Ismail Abdullahi (Metuchen, NJ: Scarecrow Press, 1992), 155.

122. Patricia Quarterman, "The Black Librarian and Academia," in *Opportunities for Minorities In Librarianship*, eds. E. J. Josey and Kenneth E. Peeples (Metuchen, NJ: Scarecrow Press, 1977), 88, 89.

123. Metro-Paterson Academy for Communications and Technology (MPACT) Report, 2008.

124. Mark Winston, in personal communication with the author, July 3, 2008.

125. Winston, in personal communication with the author, July 3, 2008.

126. Winston, in personal communication with the author, July 3, 2008.

127. Patricia Glass Schuman, "E. J. Josey as Mentor and Leader in ALA," in *E. J. Josey: An Activist Librarian*, ed. Ismail Abdullahi (Metuchen, NJ: Scarecrow Press, 1992), 28.

128. Schuman, "E. J. Josey as Mentor and Leader in ALA," 28.

129. Schuman, "E. J. Josey as Mentor and Leader in ALA," 29.

130. Barbara Ford, in personal communication with the author, April 9, 2007.

131. Association of College and Research Libraries, accessed July 4, 2019, "The ACRL Dr. E. J. Josey Spectrum Scholar Mentor Program," http://www.ala.org/acrl/membership/mentoring/joseymentoring/mentorprogram.

Chapter Six

Legacy of a Transformative Leader

Not just anyone can upstage an international icon! That is unless you're considered one in your own right. It was at the ALA Midwinter President's Program on January 13, 2008, when invited speaker Kareem Abdul-Jabbar was delivering his talk on his newly released book, *On the Shoulders of Giants: My Journey through the Harlem Renaissance,*[1] when the audience erupted into a lengthy thunderous ovation when Josey was wheeled into the room by his son-in-law, Lawrence Turner. Having been out of the spotlight for a number of years due to illness, his presence not only took spectators by surprise, but according to Turner, Abdul-Jabbar was also equally stunned and wondered who was upstaging him. Although Josey was smaller in stature compared to Abdul-Jabbar, he is considered by many a giant in the field of LIS.

Ironically, Abdul-Jabbar's discussion on the *Giants* that inspired his life included many of the same individuals who motivated Josey. He was influenced by the writings of Baldwin and the activism of King who provided perspectives for him on the civil rights movement while he was growing up.[2] Sadly, this was one of Josey's last public appearances before he passed away the following year.

Fortunately, he, along with millions, was able to witness the inauguration of America's first black president on his eighty-fifth birthday, January 20, 2009. Just like Josey, President Barack Obama rose to leadership at a time when America was undergoing a crisis. For President Obama, it was the Great Recession—a period of general economic decline detected in world markets, and especially felt in the United States, from December 2007 to June 2009. The scale and timing of the recession varied from country to country. However, it was determined by the International Monetary Fund that the overall impact of the recession was the most severe since the Great

Depression of the 1930s. As aforementioned, Josey came of age during segregation and committed his entire life fighting for civil rights. His legacy is a representation of not only the transformation that occurred in the profession, but also in the progress that was made along the lines of civil rights in the United States throughout the twentieth century. Josey's leadership and legacy are best exemplified through the countless individuals who have been inspired by his actions and in those whom he taught, fought for, and mentored in and outside of the profession.

The impact of Josey's leadership was not simply limited to the United States. His long-term involvement with IFLA and his work on the IRC afforded him the opportunity to work with many librarians across the globe. He also believed "strongly in the responsibility of library education." According to Josey, "Students in library schools should be encouraged to take courses such as International Librarianship and Comparative Librarianship."[3] It was his interest in international librarianship that led to his groundbreaking recruitment efforts of so many international students to the University of Pittsburgh LIS program in the 1980s; students like now-professor, Ismail Abdullahi (University of North Carolina Central School of Library and Information Science), who, in the festschrift he edited, wrote this:

> As one of his first Ph.D. students and his graduate assistant, I have witnessed the wealth of experience of more than thirty years in librarianship that he has brought to this institution. . . . In his teaching he tries to involve all of the students in his class in his discussion and participation . . . he uses a variety of approaches to make his students understand the relationship between librarianship and society.[4]

In the twenty-first century, African Americans and other marginalized groups are still experiencing many of the same discriminatory practices from a hundred years earlier. Racial profiling, voter suppression, mass incarceration, and shootings by overzealous police officers of unarmed African Americans are all too pervasive in today's society.[5,6] Recently, such shootings have become an everyday act of violence. In many ways, the Black Lives Matter (BLM) movement is reminiscent of the NAACP that Josey was so active in. These predominantly African American organizations support the leadership development of blacks. To this day, the NAACP continues to assist the African American community in leadership development, civil rights, and educational issues that many face. It is one of the cornerstones of African American history.

If Josey were alive today, it is likely that he would not only encourage students and librarians to be involved, but he would also be involved. It has been argued by many activists that BLM is a modern-day extension of the American civil rights movement of the 1950s and 1960s. BLM was founded in 2012 by Alicia Garza, Patrisse Cullors, and Opal Tometi after "Trayvon

Martin's 'murderer,' George Zimmerman, was acquitted for his crime, and the dead seventeen-year-old was posthumously placed on trial for his own murder."[7] Opponents of BLM have questioned if the movement infringes on their right to free speech. One example can be seen at the University of Houston in March 2016 following the Dallas shooting of police officers. The confluence of mass shootings by vigilantes and police officers and the rise of protests groups like BLM have created crises in communities and the need for public institutions like libraries to play a major role in helping communities during challenging times.

Since the founding of the American public library movement by Samuel Swett Green in 1876, libraries have been considered as safe spaces for civic engagement and public discourse. These public spaces continue to serve as centers "for debate, the exercise of rights as citizens, and a place where people of diverse backgrounds can meet as a community."[8] However, for many individuals the public library as a physical space has been more:

> A public library is free, non-judgmental, and safe. It is open evenings and weekends, centrally located, open to all ages, socioeconomic backgrounds, political and sexual orientations, and interests. It is a true public space and an ideal setting for expression of diverse opinions on political and social issues.[9]

This perception of the library as a physical space that remains open for all members of the community in times of crisis reflects a broader understanding of the library as protecting equal access and fulfilling social responsibility. When a library chooses to remain open and actively support the community with space and information through crisis (rather than closing), the library has chosen to remain nonpartisan and to actively engage with the community during difficult times. "As a physical place, the public library exemplifies the public sphere."[10] This was certainly true of the Ferguson Municipal Public Library and Baltimore's Enoch Pratt Free Library following the police shooting of Michael Brown and the death of Freddie Gray. During the weeks-long protests in both urban communities, civil unrest ensued, and each respective library remained open.[11] Two examples of Josey's legacy of leadership can be seen in Ferguson and Baltimore. In each case, library professionals have taken action amid crises.

Ferguson, Missouri, is located in what is considered a suburban town outside of the city of St. Louis.[12] The community has a long history of racial tension stemming back to the civil rights era. According to the United States Census Bureau 2017 American Community Survey (ACS), the racial makeup of the city is black 68.2 percent, white 26.6 percent, Hispanic 1.9 percent, and Asian 0.6 percent.[13] Ferguson is geographically located in the outlying areas of St. Louis County. The community is a primarily black community with approximately 23 percent of its residents living below the poverty level.[14]

On August 9, 2014, Ferguson received national and global attention in the news when Michael Brown, a young black male, was shot and killed by white police officer Darren Wilson. For about two weeks following the murder, the entire community of Ferguson was shut down, including schools and businesses. Police established curfews and deployed riot squads to maintain order, and the city was designated a national emergency. A grand jury voted not to indict Wilson in November, resulting in intensified conditions that month. The unrest sparked a vigorous debate in the United States about the relationship between law enforcement officers, African Americans, and the militarization of the police.[15]

> The circumstances around the incident and the manner in which the police handled the situation after the shooting were controversial at the time and remain so. The case ignited protests and vigils as well as looting and rioting, with skirmishes between protesters and police, on-the-scene media, and others in authority. Gov. Jay Nixon imposed curfews that were sometimes ignored and called in the National Guard.[16]

This ultimately led to the shutdown of the entire city. Nearly every public institution was closed, except for the Ferguson Municipal Public Library.[17] The Ferguson Municipal Public Library was established in June 1930 as a community library and later joined the Municipal Library of St. Louis County.[18] The library is located in the heart of Ferguson and, up until 2014, was unknown to many who lived outside of the city. The staff of the library consisted of part-time employees, volunteers, and the director of the library, Scott Bonner.[19] Although schools and most businesses were forced to close during the rioting and looting after the Wilson decision was announced, the library, with limited staffing, remained open and served as an "ad hoc school" for the people of Ferguson.[20] "The library quickly became a safe haven and expressed a peaceful resolve, becoming a critical community anchor."[21]

Bonner explained that he planned to continue building a safe space for the community in the future. "I am hoping to expand the library's offerings to better meet the public library mission of supporting continuing education, enhancing cultural literacy, and serving as a center or nexus for the commu-

Table 6.1.   Ferguson Community Statistics Based on 2010 Census

Population	20,730
Median income	$41,641
Persons in poverty	22.5%

nity itself."[22] Because of Bonner's choice to keep the library open, teachers were able to hold classes in the library, and individuals from the community were able to obtain information about housing and general information. Community members were able to gather and be in a *space* and *place* where there was calm even though there was turbulence going on directly outside the library's doors. It essentially became a safe haven to all. In an interview following the Ferguson crisis, Bonner said, "If you can keep open and keep doing what you're doing, you are going to be a safe haven."[23] In 2015, the Ferguson Municipal Public Library was named by *Library Journal* as the Gale Cengage/LJ Library of the Year for its service to Ferguson during the crisis.[24] Today, Ferguson Municipal Public Library serves as a model for other libraries around the nation. It is a great example of how libraries have become spaces where they not only provide traditional services but also have increasingly become a place of refuge for communities in the midst of crisis.

As the largest city in Maryland, Baltimore, has been dubbed "the city of neighborhoods" because of the numerous districts that are contained in the city. According to the US Census Bureau 2017 ACS, the racial makeup of the city is black 62.8 percent, white 30.3 percent, Hispanic 5.0 percent, and Asian 2.6 percent.[25]

Baltimore has a long-standing history of racial tensions that dates back to the days of Reconstruction. After the Civil War, many African Americans congregated in the city with the hopes of securing jobs. However, they were confronted by whites who feared competition, and African American labor was downgraded to unskilled or no work at all. Jim Crow laws were put into place to suppress and oppress the black citizenry. As a result, there were violent protests in 1968, which marked the beginnings of a deep divide between African Americans and the police; a divide that continues to the present. Given the racial tensions of the past, it was no surprise that the streets of Baltimore looked like a war zone in April 2015 after the funeral of Freddie Gray, a twenty-five-year-old African American man who died when he was transported in a police van after being arrested for possession of a knife. Massive protests against police brutality, some turning violent, plagued the city for days.

Protests of Gray's murder occurred near the Pennsylvania Avenue Branch of Enoch Pratt Free Library. The CVS drugstore that burned during the demonstrations was directly across the street from the library. Through it all,

Table 6.2. Ferguson Community Statistics Based on 2010 Census

Population	602,495
Median income	$46,731
Persons in poverty	22.1%

the library stayed open, a decision that received a lot of attention and praise.[26] Understanding the pivotal role that the library plays in the community as a resource, and with the Baltimore city schools closed as well as other public institutions, Melanie Townsend Diggs, Pennsylvania Avenue Branch manager and former Enoch Pratt Free Library CEO Carla Hayden, now Librarian of Congress and mentee of Josey, declared that the library would be open the next day.[27] Diggs describes what she witnessed the day after the verdict, Tuesday, April 28:

> In some ways it was a typical day, with people coming and going. But you also would have seen customers and community leaders coming in and thanking us for being open. A woman bringing us flowers, pastries. The media coming in to charge up their batteries, use the restrooms. You would have seen a young man coming in to fill out a job application online, and then coming back the next day to say that he had an interview scheduled for May 5. All of these things happened. If we had not opened our doors, we would have missed all those things.[28]

This quote by Diggs captures the sentiments of what it meant to the community to have the library remain open during this challenging time.

The Enoch Pratt Free Library is a part of the free public library system in Baltimore, Maryland. The library is one of the oldest free public library systems in United States. It serves the residents of Baltimore with locations throughout the city and serves the residents of Maryland as the State Library Resource Center. The library was established in 1882 when philanthropist Enoch Pratt offered the city of Baltimore a gift of a central library, four branch libraries, and an endowment of more than a million dollars. His objective was to establish a public circulating library that "shall be for all, rich and poor without distinction of race or color, who, when properly accredited, can take out the books if they will handle them carefully and return them."[29] The Cathedral Street Main Library is the headquarters of the entire Enoch Pratt Free Library system, which includes twenty-two community and regional branches. Up until August 2016, Hayden was the CEO of Enoch Pratt Free Library and is now the fourteenth Librarian of Congress.[30] Hayden and the staff of the Pennsylvania Avenue Branch were lauded for keeping the library open in April 2015 during the protests over the death of Freddie Gray. Hayden describes her motivation for keeping the library open:

> I knew that the libraries are community resources. I knew that they are anchors in so many communities. In a lot of communities in Baltimore, especially challenged ones, we are the only resource. If we close, we're sending a signal that we're afraid or that we aren't going to be available when times are tough. We should be open especially when times are tough.[31]

Citizens need to feel safe in their communities. Given Baltimore's history of racial tension stemming back to the 1960s, it was crucial that the Enoch Pratt Free Library remained open during this time of unrest. As a city with one of the highest crime rates in the nation, it is especially important that there are safe spaces within the city of Baltimore for people to congregate during crises. Librarians working in Baltimore and cities like Baltimore cannot afford to be passive and impartial as social issues encircle them—fortunately for Baltimore, Hayden and Diggs were strong leaders and willing to do what they felt was needed for their community.

What these examples demonstrate is the need for this type of leadership today more than ever. Although Bonner was not mentored directly by Josey, the leadership he exhibited in his library during the Ferguson crisis was very reminiscent of when Josey was director of the Savannah State College Library during the peak of the civil rights movement. They both were confronted with tough decisions on how to handle the turmoil that surrounded them. In many ways, Hayden, Josey's long-time friend and colleague, has followed in his footsteps. She served as the president of the ALA, 2003–2004, and they were on the faculty together at the University of Pittsburgh. Like Josey, Hayden believes that librarians should be actively engaged in the community. She asserts, "Librarians are activists, engaged in the social work aspect of librarianship. Now we are fighters for freedom."[32] Thus, it is not surprising that she would not only be inspired by Josey but also model his transformative leadership.

LEADERSHIP

Transformation implies a fundamental change. *Oxford English Dictionary* defines *transformation* as "the action of changing in form, shape, or appearance" or a "complete change in character."[33] *Leadership* is defined in diverse ways, but the elements commonly emphasized are to "guide," "direct," and "influence."[34] Leadership, thus, suggests not simply having power or authority but having a vision and a sense of purpose. The transformative leadership framework introduced earlier in this book and conceptualized here contends that true leadership is "transformative," effecting "alterations so comprehensive and pervasive . . . that new cultures and value systems take the place of the old."[35] A transformative leader, simply defined, is a person who can guide, direct, and influence others to bring about a fundamental change; both externally and through internal processes.[36]

In his landmark study *Leadership*, James MacGregor Burns argues that transformational leadership occurs "when one or more persons *engage* with others in such a way that leaders and followers raise one another to higher levels of motivation and morality."[37] Furthermore, he asserts that a transformational leader is one who can guide, direct, and influence others to bring about a fundamental change; both externally and through internal processes.[38] He also contends that an effective leader is a change agent because of the ability to transcend self-interest in a way that results in individual and group transformation. The characteristics that have been used to analyze Josey's leadership are: (a) idealized influence, where the leader becomes a role model; (b) inspirational motivation, where the leader provides meaning and challenge through team spirit; (c) intellectual stimulation, whereby the leader takes a creative and innovative approach to invoking change; and (d) individual consideration, where the leader serves as a mentor to those whom he or she aspires to lead. These characteristics are illustrated in figure 6.1.[39]

Each tenet of this leadership theory is important in understanding Josey's prominence as a leader. Many theorists have attempted to define leadership over the years. Bass has said, "There are almost as many different definitions of leadership as there are persons who have attempted to define the concept."[40] In her study on women's movements and organizations, Rounaq Jahan outlines several qualities of transformative leadership that, when examined with the framework by Bass, provides a lens to understanding Josey's legacy.[41] Despite the multitude of ways that leadership has been conceptualized, the following components can be identified as central to the phenomenon of leadership: (a) leadership is a process, (b) leadership involves influence, (c) leadership occurs within a group context, and (d) leadership involves goal attainment.[42]

Some scholars believe that transformative leaders are "those who are able to help others to clarify their own world view, to develop a commitment to democracy and emancipation, and to have the courage and desire to work for the empowerment of all people."[43] Peter Northouse defines *transformational leadership* as the process whereby an individual engages with others and creates a connection that raises the level of motivation and morality in both the leader and the follower. He further asserts that this type of leader is attentive to the needs and motives of followers and tries to help followers reach their fullest potential.[44] Bass offers an explanation for the use of transformational leadership in the African American community:

> "[T]he needs and experiences of the black population may dictate a greater emphasis on transformational leadership." . . . Jesse Jackson illustrated these charismatic and transformational tendencies in the 1984 and 1988 presidential election campaigns.[45]

It can also be surmised that President Obama illustrated these traits throughout his presidency. His charisma is rooted in his outstanding oratorical skills, combined with his ability to communicate complex ideas into simple messages with direct emotional appeal. One example can be seen when he was

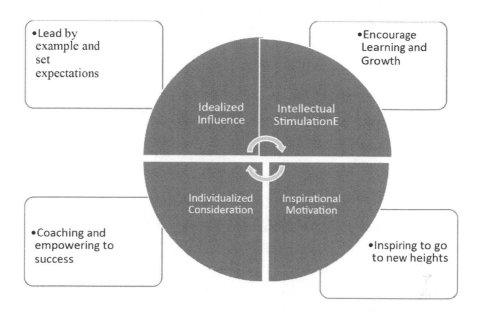

Figure 6.1. Transformational Leadership Model. *Bernard Bass*

running for president and he introduced the philosophy of "Yes We Can," which is now embedded as a motto in American tradition.

Bass further asserts:

> Leaders of black movements are characterized by their satisfaction of mutual problems and the resulting injustices. They focus much on group identity and the need for a sense of community. While leaders in the white mainstream more often direct their attention to conserving resources and the status quo, leaders of minorities, such as the blacks, must more often be transformational in their concern for social change . . . , as well as for unmet social needs for inequalities in the distribution of opportunities. [46]

Although the transformational leadership style is one more readily associated with African Americans, blacks can also be connected to other leadership theories.

On July 3, 2009, Josey passed away in Washington, North Carolina, at the age of eighty-five. He was survived by his daughter, Elaine Jacqueline Josey Turner; his brother, Robert Josey; and a host of grandchildren and great grandchildren. The funeral services held at the Cornerstone Missionary Baptist Church in Greenville, North Carolina, brought together many colleagues, librarians, and friends who celebrated his long and illustrious life. Perhaps, Josey's greatest legacy is his daughter, who was named Elaine Jacqueline Josey, to share the same initials as her dad. Her name changed after she

Table 6.3.   Characteristics of Transformational Leadership

A. Vision and commitment	B. Institutional behavior
• Equality	• Participatory
• Equity	• Egalitarian
• Empowerment	• Responsive
• Human rights	• Transparent
• Peace	• Accountable
• Sustainability	• Noncorrupt
• Shared power, responsibility, well-being	• Consensus-oriented
	• Empowering

married in college; however, she remained close to her father and became a tireless advocate for civil rights. Testimonies of Josey's leadership can be seen through his colleagues in and outside of the profession:

Al Kagan—
I can recall two examples while we served on the ALA Council together: one that I remember was just before the first gulf war, the SRRT was putting together a resolution opposing attacking IRAQ and it was a long-involved resolution; we weren't very astute about trying to get something through but more involved. But E. J. came up with a very short and sweet resolution and actually got it passed through the Council on the last day of the meeting and I remember so distinctively leaving the meeting and going to the airport and watching the TV in the airport with first President Bush announcing that he had just started to attack IRAQ. It was that same day. So that memory will always be with me. So, another example is when Ken Saro-Wiwa was the leader of the Ogoni people in the Niger Delta of Nigeria. This is the oil area, and the transnational oil companies didn't care about pollution at all. The situation there was and still is horrendous. The people formed an organization to fight for their rights and get a share of the oil revenues coming out of their region. Ken Saro-Wiwa was one of the best-known writers in the country, but the military government ruled by General Babangida didn't care at all and put him in prison along with others. I think there was a group of 80 or so arrested at the same time. They were already in jail by the time of the Commonwealth meeting. So, the Commonwealth made a statement about getting Saro-Wiwa out of jail and the response was a slap in the face, the execution of this group including Saro-Wiwa during the Commonwealth meeting. So E. J. and I and some others got together and put a resolution to the Council on boycotting Nigeria; which he was actually able to push through the Council. Only E. J. could have done that.[47]

Kathleen Weibel—
Josey's leadership style in ALA was different than his leadership style in the state library. His leadership style in the state of NY I think was sort of in between those two things. I think that was one of the things I found real intriguing about him because he was this sort of free spirit. I could not stand the NY state library, I couldn't stay and I didn't know how he does this. It was

very bureaucratic, very hierarchical, that's my view and he could manage to get things done and I suppose in some ways ALA was hierarchical bureaucratic too but because you played a role in that in a different kind of way then overall you get different types of things done. I think he's able to read situations and I think a leader needs to be able to do this. I think he can read the situation. I think he can figure out how to get done what he wants to get done and I think he can build coalitions and he can build alliances. I think people hold him in very high respect. I think part of the reason why they hold him in high respect is because of his personal dignity. It is that always wearing a suit and a tie all those things that are sort of E. J. I think you know you're in the presence of somebody who is somebody and it also that voice and I'm not taking anything away from the ideas but I think there's a passion for justice burns in him. I've been talking to people about African American involvement in the women's movement and was like where's E. J. If you needed something you went to E. J. There was no question that E. J. understood and was with you and would take care of it. He would maneuver through whatever needed to be maneuvered. So, I think that I'm not taking anything away from his single-minded agenda which I think is clear through his field; he is an African American . . . that's a clear agenda. But he's also a progressive. He's a person who sees humanity and he wants to respond to humanity, he wants social justice for his people, he wants social justice for everybody. [48]

Billie Connor, Council-at-Large, ALA 1981–1984, lobbied for Josey to be president of ALA and circulated this memo on April 13, 1983:

Dear Fellow ALA Members:

I am writing to you to ask you to vote for E. J. Josey for ALA Vice-President/President Elect in the upcoming election of ALA officers and Council for 1983–84.

E. J. has served ALA in many capacities for more than a decade: intelligent and articulate representation on the ALA Council, Executive Board membership since 1979, service on or chairmanship of many ALA and ACRL committees, and founding of the Black Caucus, of which he was the first chair in 1970.

He has been an active participant in several state library associations, has been very involved in many civic organizations, has produced nine books and more than 200 articles, has made countless speeches, and has become a role model for younger minority librarians throughout the world.

His concern for social justice and the rights of all people make him an ideal candidate in these times of the erosion of social, economic and intellectual gains of the recent past.

Our profession needs such a leader. I enthusiastically support his candidacy and hope you will also. [49]

Following Josey's successful presidential election and inspiring inaugural address, an editorial published in *Library Journal* read:

> E. J. Josey's inspiring address at his inauguration as President of the American Library Association signalled [*sic*] the culminating victory in his own long, personal struggle, often against powerful professional and political opposition. Josey's journey to become "the second librarian of African descent" elected president of ALA in 108 years is a story of unswerving service to, and battle for, ideals of social justice both in and outside of librarianship.[50]

John Berry further wrote:

> There is an important larger meaning for librarians and other Americans in the Josey challenge. . . . Josey has delivered the first battle cry in the counterattack that must become the top priority of librarians, educators, public workers, indeed all citizens for the next decade, if we are to restore and protect those institutions so basic to the health of our culture and society.[51]

From mass shootings in churches, nightclubs, and schools to protests of statutes, discrimination, and police brutality, civil unrests have become a part of our everyday life. Over the last decade, communities across the country have experienced an unpresented number of crises that have been particularly hard felt. Libraries in these towns often serve as safe spaces. However, not all libraries have risen to this challenge. Recently, a Sacramento librarian was murdered by a man who was banned from the library.[52]Occurrences of shootings like these are all too common in our society. This incident occurred on December 11, 2018, in the parking lot of the North Natomas Public Library.[53] Unfortunately, this was not the first time a senseless shooting affected the library world. Just three years earlier in June 2015, a librarian attending bible study at the Emmanuel African Methodist Episcopal Church in Charleston, South Carolina, was victim of a mass shooting when a twenty-one-year-old white supremacist murdered nine African Americans during a prayer service.[54] These incidents, much like those in the era of civil rights, highlight that there is still much to be done in regard to race relations as these are the same things that Josey was facing when he was a librarian in Savannah during civil unrest.

In the preceding chapters we have examined E. J. Josey's contributions to the LIS profession through Bass' theoretical framework of transformational leadership:

1. Individual consideration, where there is an emphasis on what a group member needs. The leader acts as a role model, mentor, facilitator, or teacher to bring a follower into the group and be motivated to do tasks.
2. Intellectual stimulation is provided by a leader in terms of challenge to the prevailing order, task, and individual. S/he seeks ideas from the group and encourages them to contribute, learn, and be independent. The leader often becomes a teacher.

3. Inspiration by a leader means giving meaning to the followers of a task. This usually involves providing a vision or goal. The group is given a reason or purpose to do a task or even be in the organization. The leader will resort to charismatic approaches in exhorting the group to go forward.

4. Idealized influence refers to the leader becoming a full-fledged role model, acting out and displaying ideal traits of honesty, trust, enthusiasm, pride, and so forth.[55]

When we consider this framework, it is apparent that Josey was a transformational leader. From his advocacy on human rights as a practitioner to recruiting and mentoring prospective students as a professor, he inspired, influenced, taught, and was a role model for generations of LIS professionals. What truly makes Josey transformative is that his contributions are very much a part of the fabric of LIS. Advocacy issues that he championed like diversity and inclusion and social justice are integral parts of the ALA policies. Students he mentored have gone on to become librarians, LIS faculty, and leaders on issues of human rights. BCALA and the other ethnic caucuses remain strong and have proven to be fervent allies for librarians of color. His publications will continue to be cited in literature. His supporters will continue his legacy by updating his publications like *The 21st-Century Black Librarian in America: Issues and Challenges.*[56]

In short, Josey transcends Bass' framework through his endless contributions and leadership. Ten years after his death, he is still celebrated in the halls of ALA and ALISE conferences. I suspect that this will continue for years to come. His legacy is enduring.

NOTES

1. Kareem Abdul-Jabbar, *On the Shoulders of Giants: My Journey through the Harlem Renaissance* (New York: Simon & Schuster, 2007).

2. "From Hoops to Ink: Kareem Abdul-Jabbar," *ilovelibraries*, September 20, 2011, http://www.ilovelibraries.org/article/hoops-ink-kareem-abdul-jabbar.

3. Ching-chih Chen, "International Relations: The Role of an Individual," in *E. J. Josey: An Activist Librarian*, ed. Ismail Abdullahi (Metuchen, NJ: Scarecrow Press, 1992), 179.

4. Ismail Abdullahi, Introduction. in *E. J. Josey: An Activist Librarian*, ed. Ismail Abdullahi (Metuchen, NJ: Scarecrow Press, 1992), xi.

5. Michelle Alexander, *The New Jim Crow: Mass Incarceration in the Age of Colorblindness*, rev. ed. (New York: The New Press, 2011).

6. Nicole D. Porter, "Politics of Black Lives Matter: Broadening Public Safety Priorities beyond Arrests and Prisons," *HuffPost*, February 13, 2015, updated April 15, 2015, http://www.huffingtonpost.com/nicole-d-porter/politics-of-black-lives-m_b_6678912.html.

7. Rick Dandes, "#BlackLivesMatter: A Guide to the Movement," accessed July 4, 2019, https://www.online-paralegal-programs.com/blacklivesmatter-movement/; *see* Black Lives Matter, "Herstory," accessed July 4, 2019, https://blacklivesmatter.com/about/herstory/.

8. Lynn A. Staeheli and Albert Thompson, "Citizenship, Community, and Struggles for Public Space," *Professional Geographer* 49, no. 1 (February 1997): 29–30, doi:10.1111/0033-0124.00053.

9. Colleen Alstad and Ann Curry, "Public Space, Public Discourse, and Public Libraries," *Libres* 13, no. 1 (March 2003): 17, https://cpb-us-e1.wpmucdn.com/blogs.ntu.edu.sg/dist/8/644/files/2014/06/Vol13_I1_pub_space.pdf.

10. Alstad and Curry, "Public Space, Public Discourse, and Public Libraries," 11.

11. John N. Berry, "2015 Gale/LJ Library of the Year: Ferguson Municipal Public Library, MO, Courage in Crisis," *Library Journal*, June 8, 2015, https://www.libraryjournal.com/?detailStory=2015-galelj-library-of-the-year-ferguson-municipal-public-library-mo-courage-in-crisis.

12. Berry, "2015 Gale/LJ Library of the Year."

13. United States Census Bureau, "QuickFacts: Ferguson City, Missouri," accessed July 4, 2019, http://www.census.gov/quickfacts/table/PST045215/2923986.

14. "QuickFacts: Ferguson City," United States Census Bureau.

15. Berry, "2015 Gale/LJ Library of the Year."

16. Berry, "2015 Gale/LJ Library of the Year."

17. Berry, "2015 Gale/LJ Library of the Year."

18. Ferguson Municipal Public Library, "History," accessed July 4, 2019, http://ferguson.lib.mo.us/about-us/history/.

19. Berry, "2015 Gale/LJ Library of the Year."

20. Berry, "2015 Gale/LJ Library of the Year;" Timothy Inklebarger, "Ferguson's Safe Haven: Library Becomes Refuge during Unrest," *American Libraries*, November 10, 2014, https://americanlibrariesmagazine.org/2014/11/10/fergusons-safe-haven/.

21. Berry, "2015 Gale/LJ Library of the Year."

22. Ingrid Conley-Abrams, "An Interview with Scott Bonner, Ferguson Librarian," *The Magpie Librarian: A Librarian's Guide to Modern Life and Etiquette*, September 3, 2014, https://magpielibrarian.wordpress.com/2014/09/03/an-interview-with-scott-bonner-ferguson-librarian/.

23. Inklebarger, "Ferguson's Safe Haven."

24. Berry, "2015 Gale/LJ Library of the Year."

25. United States Census Bureau, "QuickFacts: Baltimore City, Maryland," accessed July 4, 2019, https://www.census.gov/quickfacts/fact/table/baltimorecitymaryland,US/POP010210.

26. Megan Cottrell, "Baltimore's Library Stays Open during Unrest: Q&A with CEO Carla Hayden," *American Libraries*, May 1, 2015, https://americanlibrariesmagazine.org/blogs/the-scoop/qa-carla-hayden-baltimore/.

27. Cottrell, "Baltimore's Library Stays Open during Unrest."

28. "Melanie Townsend Diggs Receives the 2016 Lemony Snicket Prize for Noble Librarians Faced with Adversity," *ALA News*, April 12, 2016, http://www.ala.org/news/press-releases/2016/04/melanie-townsend-diggs-receives-2016-lemony-snicket-prize-noble-librarians.

29. Enoch Pratt Free Library, "About the Library: History of the Library," accessed July 4, 2019, http://www.prattlibrary.org/history/.

30. Cottrell, "Baltimore's Library Stays Open During Unrest"; Library of Congress, "About the Librarian," accessed July 4, 2019, https://www.loc.gov/about/about-the-librarian/.

31. Cottrell, "Baltimore's Library Stays Open during Unrest."

32. Catherine Orenstein, "Women of the Year 2003: Carla Diane Hayden," *Ms.* (winter 2003). Retrieved June 2016.

33. *Oxford English Dictionary*, 2nd ed., vol. 18 (Oxford: Clarendon Press, 1989), s.v. "transformation."

34. *Oxford English Dictionary*, 2nd ed., vol. 8 (Oxford: Clarendon Press), s.v. "lead"; *The Oxford English Dictionary*, 2nd ed., vol. 8 (Oxford: Clarendon Press), s.v. "leadership."

35. James MacGregor Burns, *Transforming Leadership: A New Pursuit of Happiness* (New York: Grove Press, 2003), 24–25.

36. Bernard M. Bass, "From Transactional to Transformational Leadership: Learning to Share the Vision," *Organizational Dynamics* 18, no. 3 (Winter 1990): 21, https://doi.org/10.

1016/0090-2616(90)90061-S; James MacGregor Burns, *Leadership* (New York: Harper & Row Publishers, 1978), 20.

37. Burns, *Leadership*, 20.

38. Bass, "From Transactional to Transformational Leadership," 21; Burns, *Leadership*, 20.

39. Burns, *Leadership*.

40. Bernard M. Bass, *Bass and Stogdill's Handbook of Leadership: Theory, Research, and Managerial Applications*, 3rd ed. (New York: Free Press, 1990), 11.

41. Rounaq Jahan, "Transformative Leadership in the 21st Century," (2000): 2–5, http://www.capwip.org/resources/womparlconf2000/downloads/jahan1.pdf.

42. Peter G. Northouse, *Leadership: Theory and Practice*, 5th ed. (Los Angeles: SAGE Publications, 2010), 3.

43. Richard A. Quantz, Judy Rogers, and Michael Dantley, "Rethinking Transformative Leadership: Toward Democratic Reform of Schools," *Journal of Education* 173, no. 3 (October 1991): 104, https://www.jstor.org/stable/42742231.

44. Northouse, *Leadership: Theory and Practice*, 171–91.

45. Bass, *Bass and Stogdill's Handbook of Leadership*, 746.

46. Bass, *Bass and Stogdill's Handbook of Leadership*, 746.

47. Al Kagan, personal interview with the author, April 9, 2007.

48. Kathleen Weibel, personal interview with the author, April 10, 2007.

49. Memorandum by Billie Connor, Council-at-Large, to the Council of the American Library Association, April 13, 1983.

50. John Berry, "The Josey Challenge," *Library Journal* 109, no. 12 (July 1984): 1266.

51. Berry, "The Josey Challenge," 1266.

52. "Sacramento Librarian Shot, Killed by Man Banned from the Library: Police," *KTLA 5*, December 14, 2018, https://ktla.com/2018/12/14/man-banned-from-sacramento-library-suspected-of-killing-librarian-in-targeted-attack-police/.

53. "Library Community Grieves Tragic Loss of Amber Clark of Sacramento Public Library," *ALA News*, December 21, 2018, http://www.ala.org/news/press-releases/2018/12/library-community-grieves-tragic-loss-amber-clark-sacramento-public-library.

54. "Suspected Gunman Caught in Killing of 9 at Historic Black Church in S.C.," *Chicago Tribune*, June 18, 2015, https://www.chicagotribune.com/nation-world/ct-charleston-shooting-20150617-story.html.

55. Bass, "From Transactional to Transformational Leadership," 21, https://doi.org/10.1016/0090-2616(90)90061-S; Burns, *Leadership*, 20.

56. Andrew P. Jackson, Julius C. Jefferson Jr., and Akilah S. Nosakhere, *The 21st-Century Black Librarian in America: Issues and Challenges* (Lanham, MD: Scarecrow Press, 2012).

Chronology

1924 **January** **20**	Born in Norfolk, Virginia
1940	Graduated from I. C. Norcom High School, Portsmouth, Virginia
1943–1946	Served in the United States Army
1947–1949	Attended Howard University, Washington, DC, and majors in history
1950–1952	Earned master's degree in history at Columbia University. Worked part-time in the Journalism Library at Columbia; became interested in library science as a profession after being encouraged by supervisor, Basil Miller. Joined ALA
1953–1954	Earned master's in library science at New York State University at Albany. Worked at New York State Library as technical assistant while a student. Accepted first job as librarian at the Free Public Library of Philadelphia
1954–1955	History instructor at Savannah State College
1955–1959	Director of the library and professor at Delaware State College
1957	Attended first ALA conference
1959–1966	Returned to Savannah State as director of the library. At Savannah State University Library, Josey established the Library Lecture Series, Great Books Discussion Group, National Library Week programs, developed the student NAACP student chapter

1960   Denied membership to the Georgia Library Association

1960–1966 Georgia State Youth Advisor, NAACP. Spoke before ALA
conference to congratulate ALA for adopting resolution on
individual and chapter

1962   Spoke at the ALA conference to congratulate them for
adopting a resolution that prevented discriminatory practices
toward individuals in Southern states

1962–1964 Savannah State College Libraries received the John Cotton
Dana Library Public Relations Award

1964   Drafted and submitted a resolution that won approval for a
motion that disallowed ALA staff members from attending, in
their official capacity or at the expense of the ALA, the
meetings of state associations unable to meet fully the
requirements of chapter status in the ALA. Savannah State
College Chapter, NAACP Award

1964–1965 Actions to make ALA live up to its commitments to its black
members and for the library associations in Alabama, Georgia,
Louisiana, and Mississippi to admit African Americans. ALA
ostracized segregated state associations (Alabama, Georgia,
Louisiana, and Mississippi) from official activities, and in 1965
the state associations desegregated their membership policies
and admitted Josey as the first African American member

1965   Award from the National Office of the NAACP

1965–1969 Chaired the Committee on Community Use of Academic
Libraries, Association of College and Research Libraries

1966   Accepted position of associate in the Bureau of Academic and
Research Libraries in the New York State Education
Department. Savannah Chatham County Merit Award for
Work on Economic Opportunity Task Force. Georgia NAACP
Conference Award

1966–1976 Associate/chief of the Bureau of Specialist in the Academic
and Research Libraries in New York Department of Education.
Savannah State College Award for distinguished service to
librarianship

1966   Award from *Journal of Library History* for best piece of
historical research to appear in the journal in 1969. Josey,
along with Effie Lee Morris, discussed their mutual distress
with the slowness of ALA to address African American
librarians' concerns

1968–1986 Promoted to chief, Bureau of Academic & Research Libraries at the New York State Education Department

1969–1970 Appointed to ALA Nominating Committee. Assembled black librarians for a meeting at the 1970 ALA Midwinter meeting to discuss the need to identify African American candidates and responsible white candidates to run for ALA Council in the 1971 elections; this resulted in the formation of the BCALA

1970 Elected to ALA Council. Black Caucus of ALA formed. *The Black Librarian in America* published

1971 The Black Caucus succeeded in having ALA Council pass a resolution; put ALA on the record as deploring the new private schools throughout the South avoiding integration

1972 Published *What Librarians Are Saying*

1973 Shaw University conferred honorary degree of doctor of humane letters (DHL)

1975 *New Dimensions for Academic Library Service* published by Scarecrow Press

1976–1986 Instrumental in establishing the state's 3Rs program, a regional approach to cooperative library networking geared to the needs of research and university scholars and oversaw the implementation of the New York State interlibrary loan program. Established him as a national leader in the field

1979 ALA Black Caucus Award for Distinguished Service to Librarianship

1979–1983 Moved from ALA Council to ALA executive board

1980 Received the Joseph W. Lippincott Award for his service in the ALA. The citation states, "His fervent advocacy was a major factor in eradicating racial discrimination from many library facilities and services and from a number of professional associations. As founder of the Black Caucus in ALA, and as its leader throughout the group's formative years, he gave a new strength, unity, purpose, and hope to many minority members of our profession."

1981 Elected vice president of the Albany, New York, branch of the NAACP. Led in opposing South African apartheid by spearheading protests (in Albany) with entertainers who had performed in South Africa. Received distinguished alumni award for contributions from the School of Library and Information Science at State University of New York

1982   Distinguished service award, Library Association of the City University of New York. Award for his outstanding contribution to American Librarianship and for his support of libraries and librarians of the City University of New York.

1983   Elected president of the ALA; the second black and first African American male to head the association; assuming presidency in June 1984; "Forging Coalitions for the Public Good" was the theme for his presidency

1984   Returned to executive board following his presidency

1985   Received a Capital Tribute from Congressman Major Owens and the Congressional Black Caucus Brain Trust; New York State Legislative Resolution; Ohio House of Representatives Resolution; and a US Congressional Resolution for his contribution to the profession and his leadership as ALA president

1986   NAACP President's Award, Albany Board of the NAACP Award. New York Library Association Award for significant contributions to special populations in New York State

1986–1995 Professor at the University of Pittsburgh School of Library and Information Science. Examples of courses taught: librarianship and libraries in society, management of libraries and info systems and services, library services to special populations, academic library management, politics and libraries, world librarianship, professional issues

1987   Received the doctor of public services (DPL) honoris causa from University of Wisconsin-Milwaukee. Invitation to be an advisor to Ethiopia, Zimbabwe, and Zambia on library and information science by the US government

1988   Editor of humanities, honoris causa, from North Carolina Central University

1991   Received the ALA Equality Award

1992   A festschrift in honor of his legacy in the ALA

1995   Doctor of letters degree from Clark Atlanta University

1996   Honored at the fiftieth anniversary of the ALA Washington office for his contribution to the legislative program. Awarded with the distinguished service award from the Pennsylvania Library Association

1998	John Ames Humphry Award from Forest Press and OCLC "in recognition of significant contributions to international librarianship"
1999	Honored at the celebration of the thirtieth anniversary of the Office of Intellectual Freedom for his outstanding contributions
2001	Doctor of humane letters, Clarion University of Pennsylvania
2002	Received ALA's highest award, honorary membership
2009 July 3	Died

References

Abdul-Jabbar, Kareem. *On the Shoulders of Giants: My Journey through the Harlem Renaissance*. New York: Simon & Schuster, 2007.

Abdullahi, Ismail, ed. *E. J. Josey: An Activist Librarian*. Metuchen, NJ: Scarecrow Press, 1992.

Abdullahi, Ismail. "Library Services to Multicultural Populations." In *Encyclopedia of Library and Information Science*, vol. 48, Supplement 11, edited by Allen Kent, 257–70. New York: Marcel Dekker, 1991.

Adrine, M. "Churches Traditionally Forums for Blacks." *Currents* (February 16, 1986).

Alexander, Michelle. *The New Jim Crow: Mass Incarceration in the Age of Colorblindness*. Rev. ed. New York: The New Press, 2011.

Alstad, Colleen and Ann Curry. "Public Space, Public Discourse, and Public Libraries." *Libres* 13, no. 1 (March 2003): 1–19. https://cpb-us-e1.wpmucdn.com/blogs.ntu.edu.sg/dist/8/644/files/2014/06/Vol13_I1_pub_space.pdf.

American Association of University Professors. "FAQs: Informal Glossary of AAUP Terms and Abbreviations." Accessed July 4, 2019. https://www.aaup.org/i-need-help/informal-glossary-aaup-terms-and-abbreviations.

American Association of University Professors. "1940 Statement of Principles on Academic Freedom and Tenure with 1970 Interpretive Comments." Adopted April 1970. https://www.aaup.org/file/1940%20Statement.pdf.

American Library Association. "About ALA." Accessed June 13, 2019. http://www.ala.org/aboutala/.

American Library Association. "Library Bill of Rights." Adopted June 19, 1939. Last amended January 29, 2019. http://www.ala.org/advocacy/intfreedom/librarybill.

American Library Association. "Resolution to Honor African Americans Who Fought Library Segregation." Accessed May 22, 2018. http://www.ala.org/aboutala/selection-resolutions-adopted-ala-council.

Anderson, Claud. *Black Labor, White Wealth: The Search for Power and Economic Justice*. Edgewood, MD: Duncan & Duncan, 1994.

Annual Reports of the Public Schools of Portsmouth, Virginia: School Years 1924–1925 to 1936–1937. Portsmouth, VA: National Printing Co., 1980.

Association of College and Research Libraries. "The ACRL Dr. E. J. Josey Spectrum Scholar Mentor Program." Accessed July 4, 2019. http://www.ala.org/acrl/membership/mentoring/joseymentoring/mentorprogram.

Association for Library and Information Science Education. ALISE Diversity Statement." Approved September 30, 2012. Adopted January 24, 2013. http://www. alise.org/alise---alise-diversity-statement.

Association for Library and Information Science Education. "ALISE Diversity Statement Proposal." September 22, 2012. https://www.alise.org/assets/documents/alise-diversitystatement-proposal4members.pdf.

Association for Library and Information Science Education. "ALISE Leadership Academy." Accessed June 30, 2019. https://ali.memberclicks.net/index.php?option=com_jevents&task=icalevent.detail&evid=15.

Association for Library and Information Science Education. "2017 Statistical Reports." Accessed January 15, 2019. https://www.alise.org/statistical-report-2.

Avolio, Bruce J. "Bernard (Bernie) M. Bass (1925–2007)." *American Psychologist* 63, no. 7 (October 2008): 620. doi:10.1037/0003-066x.63.7.620.

Bass, Bernard M. *Bass and Stogdill's Handbook of Leadership: Theory, Research, and Managerial Applications*. 3rd ed. New York: Free Press, 1990.

Bass, Bernard M. "From Transactional to Transformational Leadership: Learning to Share the Vision." *Organizational Dynamics* 18, no. 3 (Winter 1990): 19–31. https://doi.org/10.1016/0090-2616(90)90061-S.

Bass, Bernard M. *Leadership and Performance beyond Expectations*. New York: Free Press, 1985.

Bearman, Toni Carbo. "E. J. Josey as a Faculty Colleague." In *E. J. Josey: An Activist Librarian*, edited by Ismail Abdullahi, 149–53. Metuchen, NJ: Scarecrow Press, 1992.

Berry, John. "The Josey Challenge." *Library Journal* 109, no. 12 (July 1984): 1266.

Berry, John N. "2015 Gale/LJ Library of the Year: Ferguson Municipal Public Library, MO, Courage in Crisis." *Library Journal*. June 8, 2015. https://www.libraryjournal.com/?detailStory=2015-galelj-library-of-the-year-ferguson-municipal-public-library-mo-courage-in-crisis.

Black Caucus of the American Library Association. "Our History." Accessed December 20, 2018. https://www.bcala.org/.

Black Lives Matter. "Herstory." Accessed July 4, 2019. https://blacklivesmatter.com/about/herstory/.

Brown v. Board of Education. 347 U.S. 483 (1954).

Buckland, Michael K. "Information as Thing." *Journal of the American Society for Information Science* 42, no. 5 (June 1991): 351–60. doi:10.1002/(SICI)1097-4571.

Burns, James MacGregor. *Leadership*. New York: Harper & Row Publishers, 1978.

Burns, James MacGregor. *Transforming Leadership: A New Pursuit of Happiness*. New York: Grove Press, 2003.

Butt, Marshall W. *Portsmouth under Four Flags: 1752–1961*. Portsmouth, VA: Portsmouth Historical Association, 1961.

Chad, Barry L. "E. J. Josey, the Professor." In *E. J. Josey: An Activist Librarian*, edited by Ismail Abdullahi, 125–29. Metuchen, NJ: Scarecrow Press, 1992.

Chancellor, Renate L. "Racial Battle Fatigue: The Unspoken Burden of Black Women Faculty in LIS." *Journal of Education and Library and Information Science* 60, no. 3 (July 2019): 182–89.

Chen, Ching-chih. "International Relations: The Role of an Individual." In *E. J. Josey: An Activist Librarian*, edited by Ismail Abdullahi, 173–80. Metuchen, NJ: Scarecrow Press, 1992.

Civil Rights Act of 1964, Pub. L. No. 88–352, 78 Stat. 241.

Cleaver, Eldridge. *Soul on Ice*. New York: Dell Publishing Co., 1968.

Conley-Abrams, Ingrid. "An Interview with Scott Bonner, Ferguson Librarian." *The Magpie Librarian: A Librarian's Guide to Modern Life and Etiquette*. September 3, 2014. https://magpielibrarian.wordpress.com/2014/09/03/an-interview-with-scott-bonner-ferguson-librarian/.

Constitution and Bylaws of the Black Caucus of the American Library Association. January 21, 1970. Amended 2017. https://www.bcala.org/bylaws/.

Cora-Bramble, Denice. "Minority Faculty Recruitment, Retention and Advancement: Applications of a Resilience-Based Theoretical Framework." *Journal of Health Care for the Poor and Underserved* 17, no. 2 (May 2006): 251–55. doi:10.1353/hpu.2006.0057.

Cottrell, Megan. "Baltimore's Library Stays Open during Unrest: Q&A with CEO Carla Hayden." *American Libraries*. May 1, 2015. https://americanlibrariesmagazine.org/blogs/the-scoop/qa-carla-hayden-baltimore/.

Countryman, Matthew J. *Up South: Civil Rights and Black Power in Philadelphia*. Philadelphia: University of Pennsylvania Press, 2006.

Dandes, Rick. "#BlackLivesMatter: A Guide to the Movement." Accessed July 4, 2019. https://www.online-paralegal-programs.com/blacklivesmatter-movement/.

Davis v. City School Board, 103 F. Supp. 337 (E.D. Va. 1952), *rev'd sub nom.* Brown v. Board of Education, 349 U.S. 294 (1955).

Dawson, Alma. "Celebrating African-American Librarians and Librarianship." *Library Trends* 49, no. 1 (Summer 2000): 49–87. http://proxycu.wrlc.org/login?url=https://search-proquest-com.proxycu.wrlc.org/docview/220461892?accountid=9940.

"Delaware State University: History." Accessed November 27, 2007. http://www.desu.edu/about/history.

DeLoach, Marva L. "An African Odyssey." *Library Journal* 110, no. 4 (March 1985): 57–62.

Enoch Pratt Free Library. "About the Library: History of the Library." Accessed July 4, 2019. http://www.prattlibrary.org/history/.

Evans, Beth. "Accreditation Standards & Libraries: A Dangerous Ride down a Devolving Course." ACRLog. January 27, 2014. https://acrlog.org/2014/01/27/accreditation-standards-libraries-a-dangerous-ride-down-a-devolving-course/.

Ferguson Municipal Public Library. "History." Accessed July 4, 2019. http://ferguson.lib.mo.us/about-us/history/.

Fisher, Edith Maureen. "E. J. Josey: Library Educator." In *E. J. Josey: An Activist Librarian*, edited by Ismail Abdullahi, 130–38. Metuchen, NJ: Scarecrow Press, 1992.

Ford, Robert B. "A Pioneer in a State Library Agency: The New York Years, 1966–1986." In *E. J. Josey: An Activist Librarian*, edited by Ismail Abdullahi, 39–43. Metuchen, NJ: Scarecrow Press, 1992.

Free Library of Philadelphia. "History of the Library." Accessed June 18, 2018. http://www.library.phila.gov/about/history.htm.

"From Hoops to Ink: Kareem Abdul-Jabbar." *ilovelibraries*. September 20, 2011. http://www.ilovelibraries.org/article/hoops-ink-kareem-abdul-jabbar.

Gambrell, Kem M., Gina S. Matkin, and Mark E. Burbach. "Cultivating Leadership: The Need for Renovating Models to Higher Epistemic Cognition." *Journal of Leadership and Organization Studies* 18, no. 3 (August 2011): 308–19. http://doi.org/10.1177/1548051811404895.

Georgia Historical Society. "The Georgia Civil Rights Trail: Savannah Protest Movement Historical Marker Dedication." September 23, 2016. https://georgiahistory.com/events/savannah-protest-movement/.

Gollop, Claudia J. "Library and Information Science Education: Preparing Librarians for a Multicultural Society." *College and Research Libraries* 60, no. 4 (July 1999): 385–95.

Gray, Charles E. and John Arthur Stokes. *Above the Storm*. Hampton, VA: Four-G Publishers, 2004.

Harris, Michael H., ed. Foreword to *Melvil Dewey: His Enduring Presence in Librarianship*, edited by Sarah K. Vann, 9–10. Littleton, CO: Libraries Unlimited, 1978.

William B. Harvey, and Eugene L. Anderson. *Minorities in Higher Education: Twenty-First Annual Status Report 2003–2004*. Washington, DC: American Council on Education, February 2005.

Hewitt, Vivian D. "An Internationalist in ALA and IFLA." In *E. J. Josey: An Activist Librarian*, edited by Ismail Abdullahi, 181–93. Metuchen, NJ: Scarecrow Press, 1992.

Hicks, Deborah. "The Practice of Mentoring: Reflecting on the Critical Aspects for Leadership Development." *The Australian Library Journal* 60, no. 1 (February 2011): 66–74.

Hicks, Deborah and Lisa M. Given. "Principled, Transformational Leadership: Analyzing the Discourse of Leadership in the Development of Librarianship's Core Competences." *Library Quarterly: Information, Community, Policy* 83, no. 1 (January 2013): 7–25. doi: 10.1086/668678.

Hill's Norfolk and Portsmouth City Directory. Richmond, VA: Hill Directory Co., 1940.

Hine, Darlene Clark. "Black Professionals and Race Consciousness: Origins of the Civil Rights Movement, 1890–1950." *The Journal of American History* 89, no. 4 (March 2003): 1279–94. https://www.jstor.org/stable/3092543.

Holmes, Robert A. "Black Suffrage in the Twentieth Century." *New Georgia Encyclopedia.* Last edited June 6, 2017. https://www.georgiaencyclopedia.org/articles/government-politics/black-suffrage-twentieth-century.

Horner, Melissa. "Leadership Theory: Past, Present and Future." *Team Performance Management: An International Journal* 3, no. 4 (1997): 270–87. http://doi.org/10.1108/13527599710195402.

Hughes, Tawney A. "Idealized, Inspirational, and Intellectual Leaders in the Social Sector: Transformational Leadership and the Kravis Prize." Senior thesis, Claremont University, 2014. http://scholarship.claremont.edu/cmc/_theses/906.

Inklebarger, Timothy. "Ferguson's Safe Haven: Library Becomes Refuge During Unrest." *American Libraries.* November 10, 2014. https://americanlibrariesmagazine.org/2014/11/10/fergusons-safe-haven/.

Jackson, Andrew P., Julius C. Jefferson Jr., and Akilah S. Nosakhere, eds. *The 21st-Century Black Librarian in America: Issues and Challenges.* Lanham, MD: Scarecrow Press, 2012.

Jahan, Rounaq. "Transformative Leadership in the 21st Century." (2000): 1–13. http://www.capwip.org/resources/womparlconf2000/downloads/jahan1.pdf.

Jaeger, Paul T., John Carlo Bertot, and Renee E. Franklin. "Diversity, Inclusion, and Underrepresented Populations in LIS Research." *The Library Quarterly* 80, no. 2 (April 2010):175–81. doi: 10.1086/651053.

Jaeger, Paul T. and Renee E. Franklin. "The Virtuous Circle: Increasing Diversity in LIS Faculties to Create More Inclusive Library Services and Outreach." *Education Libraries* 30, no. 1, 20–26 (Summer 2007).

Jaeger, Paul T., Mega M. Subramaniam, Cassandra B. Jones, and John Carlo Bertot. "Diversity and LIS Education: Inclusion and the Age of Information." *Journal of Education for Library and Information Science* 52, no. 2 (July 2011): 166–83. https://idp.cua.edu/idp/profile/SAML2/POST/SSO;jsessionid=1osvugmk5pev01na23xbdav2na?execution=e1s1.

James, Rawn. *The Double V: How Wars, Protest, and Harry Truman Desegregated America's Military.* New York: Bloomsbury Press, 2013.

Jones, Clara Stanton. "E. J. Josey: Librarian for All Seasons." In *E. J. Josey: An Activist Librarian,* edited by Ismail Abdullahi, 1–20. Metuchen, NJ: Scarecrow Press, 1992.

Jones, Virginia Lacy. "A Dean's Career." In *Black Librarian in America,* edited by E. J. Josey, 19–42. Metuchen, NJ: Scarecrow Press, 1970.

Jordan, Casper LeRoy and E. J. Josey. "A Chronology of Events in Black Librarianship." In *Handbook of Black Librarianship,* edited by E. J. Josey and Ann Allen Shockley, 15–24. Littleton, CO: Libraries Unlimited, 1977.

Jordan, Casper LeRoy and E. J. Josey. "A Chronology of Events in Black Librarianship." In *Handbook of Black Librarianship,* 2nd ed., edited by E. J. Josey and Marva L. DeLoach, 3–18. Lanham, MD: Scarecrow Press, 2000.

Josey, E. J. "A College Library's Cultural Series." *Wilson Library Bulletin* 30, no. 10 (June 1956): 767–68.

Josey, E. J. "A Dreamer—with a Tiny Spark." In *The Black Librarian in America,* edited by E. J. Josey, 297–323. Metuchen, NJ: Scarecrow Press, 1970.

Josey, E. J. "A Mouthful of Civil Rights and an Empty Stomach." *Library Journal* 90, no. 2 (January 1965): 202–5.

Josey, E. J. "Black Caucus of the American Library Association." In *Handbook of Black Librarianship,* edited by E. J. Josey and Ann Allen Shockley, 66–77. Littleton, CO: Libraries Unlimited, 1977.

Josey, E. J. "College Library Accreditation: Boom or Bust." *Wilson Library Bulletin* 32, no. 3 (November 1957): 233–34.

Josey, E. J. "E. J. Josey." In *Notable Black American Men,* edited by Jessie Carney Smith, 670–72. Detroit, MI: Gale Research, 1999.

Josey, E. J. "Forging Coalitions for the Public Good." Inaugural address, American Library Association, Dallas, TX, June 27, 1984.

Josey, E. J. "Minority Representation in Library and Information Science Programs." *The Bookmark* 48, no. 1 (Fall 1989): 54–57.

Josey, E. J. "The Absent Professors." *Library Journal* 87, no. 2 (January 1962): 173–75, 181.

Josey, E. J. "The Challenges of Cultural Diversity in the Recruitment of Faculty and Students from Diverse Backgrounds." *Journal of Education for Library and Information Science* 34, no. 4 (Fall 1993): 302–11. https://www.jstor.org.proxycu.wrlc.org/stable/41308876.

Josey, E. J. "The Civil Rights Movement and American Librarianship: The Opening Round." In *Activism in American Librarianship, 1962–1973*, edited by Mary Lee Bundy and Frederick J. Stielow, 13–20. New York: Greenwood Press, 1987.

Josey, E. J. "The Future of the Black College Library." *Library Journal* 94, no. 16 (September 1969): 3019–22.

Josey, E. J. "The Role of the College Library Staff in Instruction in the Use of the Library." *College and Research Libraries* 23, no. 6 (November 1962): 492–98. https://doi.org/10.5860/crl_23_06_492.

Josey, E. J., ed. *The Black Librarian in America*. Metuchen, NJ: Scarecrow Press, 1970.

Josey, E. J., ed. *The Black Librarian in America Revisited*. Metuchen: NJ: Scarecrow Press, 1994.

Josey, E. J., ed. *What Black Librarians Are Saying*. Metuchen, NJ: Scarecrow Press, 1972.

Josey, E. Junius. "The College Library and the Atom." *Library Journal* 83, no. 9 (May 1958): 1341–43.

Josey, E. J. and Marva L. DeLoach. "Discrimination and Affirmative Action: Concerns for Black Librarians and Library Workers." In *Librarians' Affirmative Action Handbook*, edited by John H. Harvey and Elizabeth M. Dickinson, 177–99. Metuchen, NJ: Scarecrow Press, 1983.

Josey, E. J. and Marva L. DeLoach, eds. *Handbook of Black Librarianship*. 2nd ed. Lanham, MD: Scarecrow Press, 2000.

Josey, E. J. and Ann Allen Shockley, eds. *Handbook of Black Librarianship*. Littleton, CO: Libraries Unlimited, 1977.

Kagan, Al. "ALA, IFLA, and South Africa." *Progressive Librarian: A Journal for Critical Studies and Progressive Politics in Librarianship* 46 (Winter 2017/2018): 63–85. http://www.progressivelibrariansguild.org/PL/PL46/063kagan.pdf.

King, Thomas Lawrence. "Support for Human Rights in Librarianship: The Legacy of E. J. Josey." In *E. J. Josey: An Activist Librarian*, edited by Ismail Abdullahi, 89–106. Metuchen, NJ: Scarecrow Press, 1992.

Kniffel, Leonard. "To Be Black and a Librarian: Talking with E. J. Josey." *American Libraries* 31, no. 1 (January 2000): 80, 82. https://www.jstor.org/stable/25637460.

Knowlton, Steven A. "Three Decades since *Prejudices and Antipathies*: A Study of Changes in the Library of Congress Subject Headings." *Cataloging and Classification Quarterly* 40, no. 2 (2005): 123–45. https://doi.org/10.1300/J104v40n02_08.

Kotter, John P. *Leading Change*. Boston, MA: Harvard Business Review Press, 2012.

Lacy, Meagan and Andrea J. Copeland. "The Role of Mentorship Programs in LIS Education and in Professional Development." *Journal of Education for Library and Information Science* 54, no. 2 (April 2013): 135–46.

Landgraf, Greg. "Blazing Trails: Pioneering African-American Librarians Share Their Stories." *American Libraries*. January 2, 2018. https://americanlibrariesmagazine.org/2018/01/02/blazing-trails/.

Latson, Jennifer. "How America's First Self-Made Female Millionaire Built Her Fortune." *Time*. December 24, 2014. http://time.com/3641122/sarah-breedlove-walker/.

Levine, Lawrence W. *The Unpredictable Past: Explorations in American Cultural History*. New York: Oxford University Press, 1993.

Levitt, Steven D. "Let's Just Get Rid of Tenure (Including Mine)." *Freakonomics*. March 3, 2007. http://freakonomics.com/2007/03/03/lets-just-get-rid-of-tenure/.

Lewis, Earl. *In Their Own Interests: Race, Class, and Power in Twentieth-Century Norfolk, Virginia*. Berkeley: University of California Press, 1991.

"Library Community Grieves Tragic Loss of Amber Clark of Sacramento Public Library." *ALA News*. December 21, 2018. http://www.ala.org/news/press-releases/2018/12/library-community-grieves-tragic-loss-amber-clark-sacramento-public-library.

Library of Congress. "About the Librarian." Accessed July 4, 2019. https://www.loc.gov/about/about-the-librarian/.

Library of Congress. "NAACP: A Century in the Fight for Freedom: Founding and Early Years." Accessed June 20, 2019. https://www.loc.gov/exhibits/naacp/founding-and-early-years.html.

"Library Pioneer Dr. E. J. Josey Saluted during American Library Association Annual Confab," *Jet* 88, no. 10 (July 1995): 33.

Library Services and Technology Act, Pub. L. 94–462, tit. II, subtit. B, as added Pub. L. No. 104–208, div. A, tit. I, sec. 101(e) [tit. VII, sec. 702], 110 Stat. 3009–233, 3009–295 (1996).

Lumumba, Malikah Dada. "E. J. Josey: A Mentor and Friend." In *E. J. Josey: An Activist Librarian*, edited by Ismail Abdullahi, 154–66. Metuchen, NJ: Scarecrow Press, 1992.

Martin, Robert Sidney and Orvin Lee Shiflett. "Hampton, Fisk, and Atlanta: The Foundations, the American Library Association, and Library Education for Blacks, 1925–1941." *Libraries and Culture* 31, no. 2 (Spring 1996): 299–325. https://www.jstor.org/stable/25548438.

McCoy, Jim F. "Remembrances and Reflections of an NAACP Leader." In *E. J. Josey: An Activist Librarian*, edited by Ismail Abdullahi, 121–24. Metuchen, NJ: Scarecrow Press, 1992.

McShane, Steven L. and May Ann Von Glinow. *Organizational Behavior: Emerging Knowledge and Practice for the Real World*. 5th ed. Boston, MA: McGraw-Hill/Irwin, 2010.

"Melanie Townsend Diggs Receives the 2016 Lemony Snicket Prize for Noble Librarians Faced with Adversity." *ALA News*. April 12, 2016. http://www.ala.org/news/press-releases/2016/04/melanie-townsend-diggs-receives-2016-lemony-snicket-prize-noble-librarians.

"Memo to Members." *ALA Bulletin* 50, no. 7 (July–August 1964): 592–93. https://www.jstor.org/stable/i25696961.

Memorandum by Allen Kent to the Faculty and Staff at the University of Pittsburgh School of Library and Information Science. 1986.

Memorandum by Billie Connor, Council-at-Large, to the Council of the American Library Association. April 13, 1983.

Metro-Paterson Academy for Communications and Technology (MPACT) Report, 2008.

Moon, Eric. "A 'Chapter' Chapter: E. J., ALA, and Civil Rights." In *E. J. Josey: An Activist Librarian*, edited by Ismail Abdullahi, 44–52. Metuchen, NJ: Scarecrow Press, 1992.

Moreillon, Judi. "Educating for School Library Leadership: Developing the Instructional Partnership Role." *Journal of Education for Library and Information Science* 54, no. 1 (January 2013): 55–66. https://www.jstor.org.proxycu.wrlc.org/stable/43686932.

Mount Hermon Reunion. *Fighting Spirit Forever 1990*. Portsmouth, VA: Mount Hermon Souvenir Journal Committee, 1990.

Nadler, David A. and Michael L. Tushman. *Competing by Design: The Power of Organizational Architecture*. New York: Oxford University Press, 1997.

National Archives and Records Administration. "United States World War II Army Enlistment Records, 1938–1946." In *FamilySearch*. Accessed April 12, 2010. https://familysearch.org/search/collection/results?count=20&query=%2Bgivenname%3AElonnie~%20%2Bsurname%3AJosey~%20%2Brace%3ABlack&collection_id=2028680.

National Center for Education Statistics. U.S. Department of Education. *The Condition of Education 2017*. May 2017. https://nces.ed.gov/pubsearch/pubsinfo.asp?pubid=2017144.

Neigel, Christina. "LIS Leadership and Leadership Education: A Matter of Gender." *Journal of Library Administration* 55, no. 7 (October 2015): 521–34. https://doi.org/10.1080/01930826.2015.1076307.

Newby-Alexander, Cassandra, Mae Breckenridge-Haywood, and African American Historical Society of Portsmouth. *Black America Series: Portsmouth Virginia*. Charleston, SC: Arcadia Publishing, 2003.

Newton, James E. "Black Americans in Delaware: An Overview." Accessed July 30, 2018. http://www1.udel.edu/BlackHistory/overview.html.

Northouse, Peter G. *Leadership: Theory and Practice*. 5th ed. Los Angeles: SAGE Publications, 2010.

"Notes and Asides at an International Conference." *American Libraries* 16, no. 9 (October 1985): 615. https://www.jstor.org/stable/25629740.

"Number of Inhabitants—Virginia." In United States Bureau of the Census. *Census of Population: 1960*, vol. 1, *Characteristics of the Population*, pt. 48, *Virginia*. Washington, DC: Government Printing Office, 1963. https://www2.census.gov/prod2/decennial/documents/09768066v1p48ch2.pdf.

Oxford English Dictionary. s.v. "mentor (*n.*)." Accessed June 20, 2019. https://www.oed.com/view/Entry/116575?rskey=Zgz5Z2&result=1#eid.

Paris, Marion. "Why Library Schools Fail." *Library Journal* 115, no. 16 (October 1990): 38–42.

Peterson, Lorna. "Alternative Perspectives in Library and Information Science: Issues of Race." *Journal of Education for Library and Information Science* 37, no. 2 (Spring 1996): 163–74. https://www.jstor.org/stable/40324271.

Peterson, Lorna. "The Definition of Diversity: Two Views—A More Specific Definition." *Journal of Library Administration* 27, nos. 1–2 (May 1999): 17–26. https://doi.org/10.1300/J111v27n01_03.

"The Philosophy and Opinions of Marcus Garvey or Africa for the Africans." In *Philosophy and Opinions of Marcus Garvey*, ed. Amy Jacques-Garvey, with an introduction by Robert A. Hill. New York: Atheneum, 1992. First published 1923–1925 by Amy Jacques-Garvey.

Plessy v. Ferguson, 163 U.S. 537 (1896), *overruled by* Brown v. Board of Education, 347 U.S. 483 (1954).

Porter, Nicole D. "Politics of Black Lives Matter: Broadening Public Safety Priorities beyond Arrests and Prisons." *HuffPost*. February 13, 2015. Updated April 15, 2015. http://www.huffingtonpost.com/nicole-d-porter/politics-of-black-lives-m_b_6678912.html.

Quantz, Richard A., Judy Rogers, and Michael Dantley. "Rethinking Transformative Leadership: Toward Democratic Reform of Schools." *Journal of Education* 173, no. 3 (October 1991): 96–118. https://www.jstor.org/stable/42742231.

Quarterman, Patricia. "The Black Librarian and Academia." In *Opportunities for Minorities in Librarianship*, edited by E. J. Josey and Kenneth E. Peeples, 87–94. Metuchen, NJ: Scarecrow Press, 1977.

Richardson, John V. "History of American Library Science: Its Origins and Early Development." In *Encyclopedia of Library and Information Sciences*. 3d erd. 2010: 1 9. doi: 10.1081/E-ELIS3-120043738.

Roden, C. B. "Report of the Committee on Racial Discrimination." *Bulletin of the American Library Association* 31, no. 1 (January 1937): 37–38.

Rubin, Richard E. *Foundations of Library and Information Science*. 4th ed. Chicago: Neal-Schuman, 2016.

"Sacramento Librarian Shot, Killed by Man Banned from the Library: Police." *KTLA 5*. December 14, 2018. https://ktla.com/2018/12/14/man-banned-from-sacramento-library-suspected-of-killing-librarian-in-targeted-attack-police/.

Savannah State University 2005–2007 Catalog. Savannah, GA: Savannah State University. 2005. https://www.savannahstate.edu/academic-affairs/documents/catalog05-07undergraduate.pdf.

Saye, Albert B. *Georgia: History and Government*. Rev. Teacher's ed. Austin, TX: Steck-Vaughn Company, 1982.

Schuman, Patricia Glass. "E. J. Josey as Mentor and Leader in ALA." In *E. J. Josey: An Activist Librarian*, edited by Ismail Abdullahi, 27–31. Metuchen, NJ: Scarecrow Press, 1992.

"Segregation and ALA Membership." *Wilson Library Bulletin* 36, no. 7 (March 1962): 558–61, 579.

"Sleep No More at IFLA: Report on the International Federation of Library Associations & Institutions 51st Council and General Conference, August 18–24, Chicago, U.S.A." *American Libraries* 16, no. 9 (October 1985): 610–12, 164–15, 617–18. https://www.jstor.org/stable/25629740.

Smith, Alonzo. "Howard University (1867–)." BlackPast. February 8, 2010. http://www.blackpast.org/aah/howard-university-1867.

Speller, Benjamin F. "E. J. Josey: A True Friend of North Carolina Central University." In *E. J. Josey: An Activist Librarian*, edited by Ismail Abdullahi, 139–48. Metuchen, NJ: Scarecrow, Press, 1992.

St. Lifer, Evan and Corinne Nelson. "Unequal Opportunities: Race Does Matter." *Library Journal* 122, no. 18 (November 1997): 42–46. http://proxycu.wrlc.org/login?url=https://search-proquest-com.proxycu.wrlc.org/docview/196736670?accountid=9940.

Staeheli, Lynn A. and Albert Thompson. "Citizenship, Community, and Struggles for Public Space." *Professional Geographer* 49, no. 1 (February 1997): 28–38. doi:10.1111/0033-0124.00053.

Stamberg, Susan. "How Andrew Carnegie Turned His Fortune into a Library Legacy." August 1, 2013. https://www.npr.org/2013/08/01/207272849/how-andrew-carnegie-turned-his-fortune-into-a-library-legacy.

"Suspected Gunman Caught in Killing of 9 at Historic Black Church in S.C." *Chicago Tribune.* June 18, 2015. https://www.chicagotribune.com/nation-world/ct-charleston-shooting-20150617-story.html.

"The Philosophy and Opinions of Marcus Garvey or Africa for the Africans." In *Philosophy and Opinions of Marcus Garvey*, ed. Amy Jacques-Garvey, with an introduction by Robert A. Hill. New York: Atheneum, 1992. First published 1923–1925 by Amy Jacques-Garvey.

Thomas, Lucille. "E. J. Josey, the 101st President of the American Library Association." In *E. J. Josey: An Activist Librarian*, edited by Ismail Abdullahi, 21–26. Metuchen, NJ: Scarecrow Press, 1992.

Thomison, Dennis. *A History of the American Library Association, 1876–1972*. Chicago, IL: American Library Association, 1978.

Tucker, John Mark, ed. *Untold Stories: Civil Rights, Libraries, and Black Librarianship*. Champaign: University of Illinois Graduate School of Library and Information Science, 1998.

United States Bureau of the Census. *Historical Statistics of the United States, Colonial Times to 1957*. Washington, DC, 1960. https://www.census.gov/library/publications/1960/compendia/hist_stats_colonial-1957.html.

United States Census Bureau. "1930 United States Census Population Statistics." Accessed November 9, 2007. http://search.ancestrylibrary.com/cgi-bin.sse.dll?db=1930usfedcen.

United States Census Bureau. "QuickFacts: Baltimore City, Maryland." Accessed July 4, 2019. https://www.census.gov/quickfacts/fact/table/baltimorecitymaryland,US/POP010210.

United States Census Bureau. "QuickFacts: Ferguson City, Missouri." Accessed July 4, 2019. http://www.census.gov/quickfacts/table/PST045215/2923986.

Vann, Sarah K., ed. *Melvil Dewey: His Enduring Presence in Librarianship*. Littleton, CO: Libraries Unlimited, 1978.

Wedgeworth, Robert. "ALA and the Black Librarian: Strategies for the '70's." In *Black Librarian in America*, edited by E. J. Josey, 69–76. Metuchen, NJ: Scarecrow Press, 1970.

Whitmire, Ethelene. "Breaking the Color Barrier: Regina Andrews and the New York Public Library." *Libraries and the Cultural Record* 42, no. 4 (2007): 409–21. doi:10.1353/lac2007.0068.

Whitmire, Ethelene. *Regina Anderson Andrews: Harlem Renaissance Librarian*. Urbana: University of Illinois Press, 2014.

Wiegand, Wayne A. *The Politics of an Emerging Profession: The American Library Association, 1876–1917*. New York: Greenwood Press, 1986.

Wiegand, Wayne A. and Shirley A. Wiegand. *The Desegregation of Public Libraries in the Jim Crow South: Civil Rights and Local Activism*. Baton Rouge: Louisiana State University Press, 2018.

William R. and Norma B. Harvey Library. "Research Guides: The Hampton University Forum on Minority Recruitment and Retention in the LIS Field: University History in Training of Minority Librarians." Last updated October 1, 2018. https://hamptonu.libguides.com/c.php?g=815577&p=5832646.

Williams, Chad. "African Americans and World War I." African and African Diasporan Transformations in the 20th Century, Schomburg Center for Research in Black Culture, New York Public Library. Accessed May 22, 2018. http://exhibitions.nypl.org/africanaage/essay-world-war-i.html.

World Encyclopedia of Library and Information Services. Chicago: American Library Association, 1993. s.v. "Gleason, Eliza Atkins."

Wright, Joyce C. "Recruiting Minorities to the Profession." In *E. J. Josey: An Activist Librarian*, edited by Ismail Abdullahi, 167–72. Metuchen, NJ: Scarecrow Press, 1992.

Index

About the Author

Renate L. Chancellor is associate professor of library and information science at Catholic University of America in Washington, DC. She received her master's and PhD in information studies from UCLA. Her research focuses on human information behavior and social justice in library and information science.

She has published articles in journals including *Journal of History and Culture*, *The Law Library Journal*, and the *Journal of Education for Library and Information Science*. Dr. Chancellor has also published articles on libraries as pivotal community spaces in times of crises, digital rights management, and intellectual property rights law. As the head of the law librarianship program of study, she teaches several courses, including, but not limited to, legal research, the information professions in society, human information behavior, oral history, and visions of Italy.

Professionally active in the Association for Library and Information Science Education (ALISE), the American Library Association (ALA), and several other professional library organizations, Dr. Chancellor is the recipient of the 2012 ALISE/Norman Horrocks Leadership Award and the 2014 ALISE Excellence in Teaching Award.